Praise for My Orange Duffel Bag

"In this one-of-a-kind book, Sam Bracken lays out a step-by-step approach to change through sharing his own remarkable journey from victim to conqueror. This book is a must-read for everyone who wants to leave their baggage behind once and for all and become the change they seek!"

–STEPHEN R. COVEY, author of *The 7 Habits of Highly Effective People*, *The 8th Habit: From Effectiveness to Greatness* and *The 3rd Alternative*

"I spent five years with Sam Bracken at a time of transformation for him. His is a stunning story of courage, resiliency, and servant-leadership. We would all do well to read and heed his powerful message."

–BILL CURRY, NCAA football coach and former NFL player

"Sam Bracken is a shining example of the transformational power of education. A caring teacher looked closely enough at his life to take away his barrier to learning. That simple act launched Sam on his journey out of poverty."

–RUBY PAYNE, Ph.D., author of the bestsellers
A Framework for Understanding Poverty and
Bridges Out of Poverty: Strategies for Professionals and Communities

"If you want to make big changes in your own life, but aren't sure how, please read this book."

–SEAN COVEY, author of *The 7 Habits of Highly Effective Teens* and *The 6 Most Important Decisions You'll Ever Make: A Guide for Teens*

"In Sam Bracken's simple, unique, and poignant telling of his life story, he manages to take away all excuses and inspire readers to move past the valleys of hurts and disappointments in their lives."

–RICHARD PAUL EVANS, #1 *New York Times* bestselling author of *The Christmas Box*

"This is the must-read book of the year. It represents everything I believe in."

–KATHY L. PATRICK, founder of the world's largest book club The Pulpwood Queens, which named this book the November 2010 Book Selection

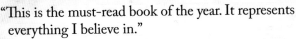

"In *My Orange Duffel Bag* Sam Bracken not only shares his remarkable story of overcoming life's problems but teaches all of us how we can do the same. From desire to gratitude this book will touch your heart and change your life."

–CHESTER ELTON, co-author of *The Carrot Principle*

SAM BRACKEN

My ORANGE Duffel Bag

a Journey to Radical Change

brought to life by
Echo Garrett

CROWN
ARCHETYPE
New York

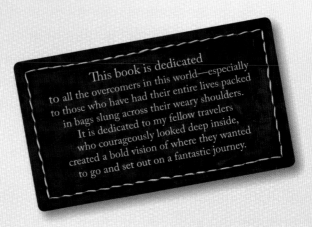

This book is dedicated
to all the overcomers in this world—especially
to those who have had their entire lives packed
in bags slung across their weary shoulders.
It is dedicated to my fellow travelers
who courageously looked deep inside,
created a bold vision of where they wanted
to go and set out on a fantastic journey.

Copyright © 2010 by Samuel Ray Bracken, Echo Montgomery Garrett, and Raymond John Kuik

All rights reserved.

Published in the United States by Crown Archetype, an imprint of the Crown Publishing Group, a division of Random House, Inc., New York.

www.crownpublishing.com

Crown Archetype with colophon is a trademark of Random House, Inc.

Originally published in the United States by Operation Orange Media, LLC, Kaysville, Utah, in 2010.

Library of Congress Cataloging-in-Publication Number: 2010924973

ISBN 978-0-307-98488-3
eISBN 978-0-307-98489-0

Printed in China

Book design by The FaQtory
Photograph and illustration credits appear on page 203.
Cover design by Laura Duffy
Cover zipper: Barry David Marcus
Cover photos, spine, counterclockwise from top left: Getty Images, iStockphoto, Photos.com, Photos.com, iStockphoto, Getty Images, Kevin Garrett. Back cover photo: Kevin Garrett

10 9 8 7 6 5 4 3 2 1

First Crown Archetype Edition

This is the story of my life. It chronicles the pain I suffered. Yet I survived all manner of abuse, because caring teachers, coaches and friends reached out to me and guided me to direct my energies toward positive goals. I learned to forgive and let love transform my thoughts and actions. The steps I took will help you make radical changes in your life. You can use what I call my "7 Rules for the Road" to set your course.

May your journey take you to a place even beyond your greatest hopes.

—Sam Bracken

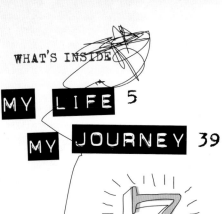

"The lights distort from the distance and heat, we are let down by the people we believe. Yes, it is true sometimes life can be tough, but I still believe you can pull me through with your love. Yeah, yes, you are something. Fear nothing."

ARTIST/SONGWRITER:
KEVIN MONTGOMERY

BORN:
The product of a rape
UNWANTED

AGE 3

Always hungry. Strange men come in and out of our apartment, but never stay.

A bad man steals everything even the food out of our fridge.

Mommy cries. So do Gerry and Sissy, my little brother and baby sister.

DON'T CRY

AGE 4

Left with nuns at an orphanage. Mommy comes back for us.

DON'T LEAVE

AGE 5

My left arm is doused in lighter fluid by an older boy. He flicks the lighter. I'm on fire. I dip my arm in a creek. He laughs.

We move to Las Vegas.

DON'T TELL

Bracken

AGE 7

Mom marries Leroy Bracken. Leroy has
kids, too. I practice writing my new
last name at school.

The older boy is now my stepbrother.

FEAR

11

AGE 8

Mom has three jobs.
She's gone all the time.
She takes pills to help her stay awake.

Leroy watches TV in his underwear.
He always has a beer in his hand.
When Leroy gets angry, he hits.
He is angry a lot.
I never know why I get beaten.

12

My older stepbrother
and stepsisters smoke
weed and do drugs.
Mom and Leroy don't mind.

Sometimes they join them.

UNSPEAKABLE ABUSE

13

AGE 9

My older stepbrother and stepsisters take me with them to parties all the time. They give me beer, booze and teach me how to use a bong.

My little brother and I get arrested for stealing a dog whistle for my new puppy. We ride home in the back of a police car.

CHAOS

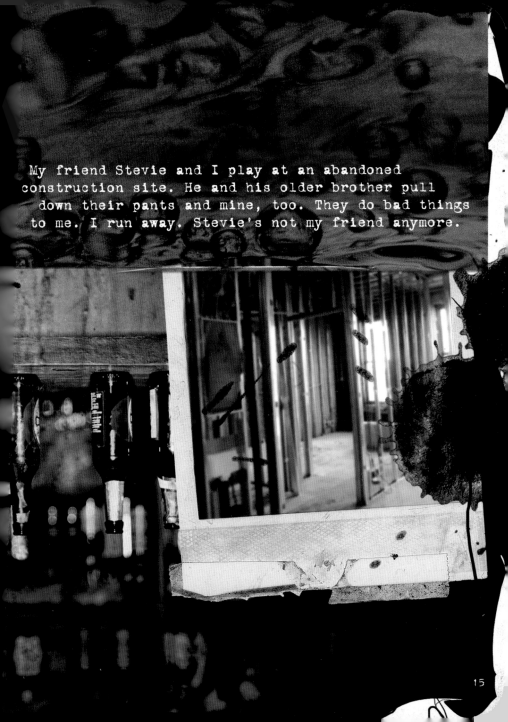

My friend Stevie and I play at an abandoned
construction site. He and his older brother pull
down their pants and mine, too. They do bad things
to me. I run away. Stevie's not my friend anymore.

AGE 10

Leroy takes me to my first track meet.
I win three gold medals and break the
state record in the 880 yard race.

Running makes me feel GOOD.
    I run
        and run
            and run in the desert.

I get a bed to sleep on.

                My stepbrother Lenny uses
                    me as a human dart board.

TRAPPED

AGE 11
Lenny steals my mom's station wagon and
all the money from her catering business.

We lose the business and our house.

My new best friend Tommy's dad is a mobster.
His dad keeps silver dollars from the casinos
in giant fish bowls in their apartment.
He lets us take fistfuls for candy and
pinball at the corner 7-Eleven™.

I get bused to school across town.

DON'T ASK WHY

AGE 12

Mom takes us with her to work at the casino.
We sit in a corner and watch the comedians,
singers and dancers. I like the comedians best,
because I like to laugh. Sometimes Mom sneaks
us screwdrivers - orange juice and vodka.

I stash a collection of 20 bongs in
a secret drawer under my bed.

Mom finds my stash of weed.
She asks if she can have some.
"Sure," I say. "Help yourself."

MADNESS

AGE 13

I grow so big that I can gamble and get free drinks at the casinos. I look like a man, but inside I still feel like a little boy.

For my birthday, my stepdad tells Lenny to find a hooker for me to celebrate becoming a man. I beg Lenny to take the $60 and leave me alone. He does.

One day Tommy and his father disappear.
I never see them again.
I'm lonely with Tommy gone.

I get a new girlfriend. She is 21 years old.

I collapse at track practice
after a party binge with Lenny.

Crawling in the dirt, I make a
decision: I refuse to be like my family.
No more
drugs,
drinking
and craziness.

NOT LIKE THEM

AGE 14

One of my teachers figures out I need glasses.
No more special ed classes.
My grades go from Cs, Ds and Fs to As.

That summer I go to my first football camp
in California. Mom gives me an orange
duffel bag with my name on it.

I play on the freshman, junior varsity and
varsity football teams as a freshman.
I get into the state championship game.

We win.

Lenny kills my stepdad Leroy's best friend,
an ex-con who's been living with us.
Lenny runs off with the guy's 17-year-old
girlfriend. The cops catch them in Texas.

We visit Lenny on weekends
in a boys' work camp.

Leroy is accused of molesting my little sister.
Mom and my stepdad split up.

DENIAL

25

AGE 15

Mom kicks me out
of our apartment
and moves in with
the Hessians
motorcycle gang.
When the Mob
doesn't want to
do a hit, the
Hessians are the
hired guns.
She embroiders
elaborate designs
for their jackets.
Mom's kind of like
their den mother.

ABANDONED

27

AGE 16

I take my orange duffel bag and go live with my best friend's family. Is this what normal feels like?

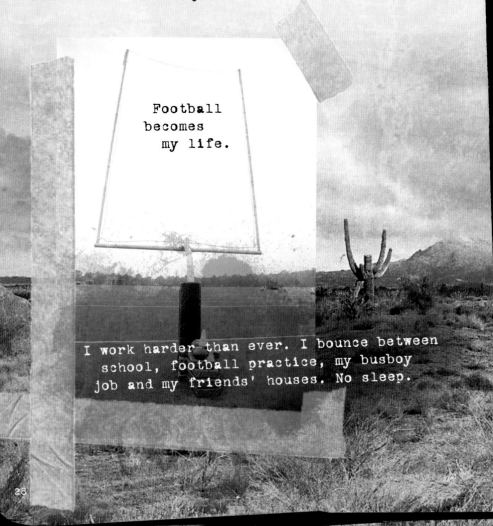

Football
becomes
my life.

I work harder than ever. I bounce between school, football practice, my busboy job and my friends' houses. No sleep.

Mom has a mental breakdown.

I visit her in the desert where she's staked
her claim to a long ago abandoned gold mine.
    Sometimes she stays in a dirt-floor shack,
warming herself by a potbellied stove.

        She feeds me dumpster stew and
        tells me who my real father is.

I start looking for God.

DESPAIR

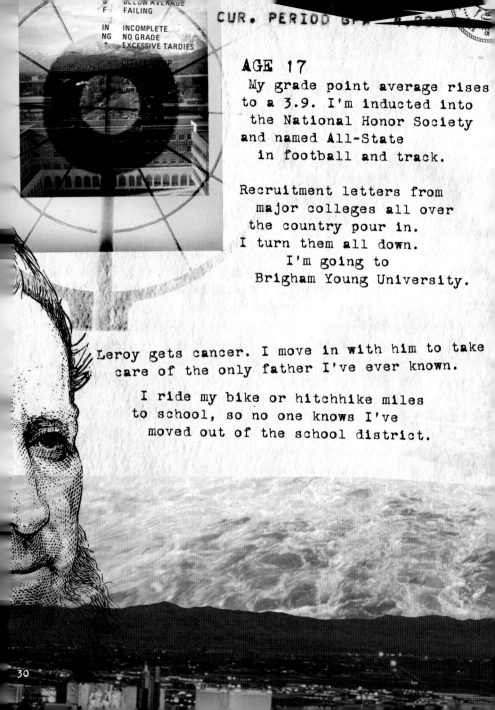

AGE 17

My grade point average rises
to a 3.9. I'm inducted into
the National Honor Society
and named All-State
in football and track.

Recruitment letters from
major colleges all over
the country pour in.
I turn them all down.
I'm going to
Brigham Young University.

Leroy gets cancer. I move in with him to take
care of the only father I've ever known.

I ride my bike or hitchhike miles
to school, so no one knows I've
moved out of the school district.

4209 COTTAGE CR

LAS VEGAS, NEV.   89109

LEADERSHIP

IS PRESENTED TO

Samuel Bro

I work as a busboy at a casino
restaurant on the Strip at night
and give Leroy the money.

I get baptized.

Leroy dies.

31

Right before my graduation,
I find out my football scholarship
at BYU has gone to someone else.
That's okay. I'll just walk on.

Summer comes and I move to Provo, Utah. I do
construction and workout with the team at BYU.

I come home to Las Vegas to play in an
All-Star game and blow out my knee.

My gridiron dreams slip away.

I pray.

My doctor tells me my knee will be fine.

"Boy, let's get your films together.
    You are too smart and too good
a football player to give up now."

The good doc helps me send out letters
with my films to top football schools with
good academic programs around the country.

        A MIRACLE

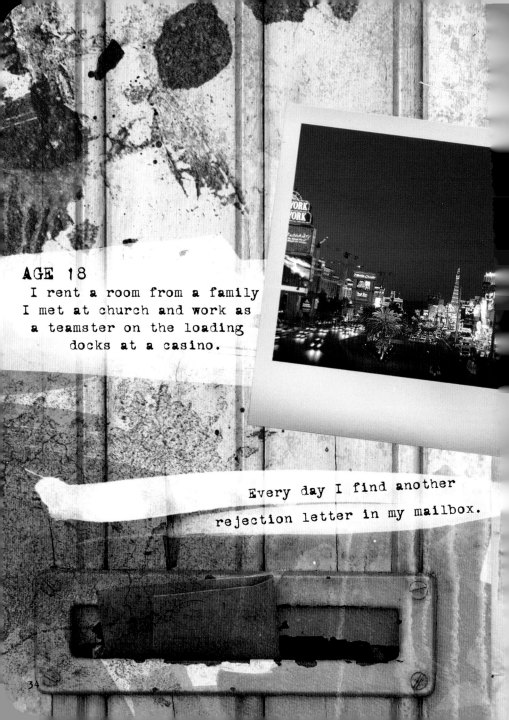

AGE 18

I rent a room from a family
I met at church and work as
a teamster on the loading
docks at a casino.

Every day I find another
rejection letter in my mailbox.

Then one day, the phone rings.
On the other end of the
line is Coach Ken Blair from
Georgia Tech in Atlanta:

"Son, we like what we see on your films,
and we'd like you to come visit us."

NCAA AWARD

GEORGIA INSTITUTE OF TECHNOLOGY
Atlanta, Georgia 30332

WANTED

TO: Samuel R. Bracken   Sport: FOO'

Box 32867
GEORGIA TECH

Atlanta, GA 30332

This is to inform you that your NCAA Award will be renewed for the 198
below:

35

Fall Quarter ___ X ___   Winter Quarter ___ X ___   Sp

I've been on an airplane once before.
I meet Coach Bill Curry in Atlanta, and he
offers me a full ride football scholarship.

So that's what it feels like - having
some place to go and having someone
want you to be there.

When I leave Las Vegas, I take my
orange duffel bag, and I put the only
extra pair of jeans I own, a couple
of T-shirts and my underwear
in that bag. I pack it with all
my hopes and dreams and fly away.

SAM
BRACKEN

Surgery
ard
rgery

By Thomas M. Stinson
Staff Writer

A stepdance at right guard, where Georgia Tech has spent four weeks this spring looking for a leading partner, took an unforeseen turn Wednesday.

Starter-designate Sam Brack-en underwent shoulder surgery to shore up a previous injury leav-

spot in the offensive line because there is not an established starter there," said offensive line coach Mac McWhorter.

Bracken, a fifth-year senior from Las Vegas, Nev., was operated on by team orthodpedist Fred Allman, who removed a piece of surgical screw that had broken off in his left shoulder.

The screw had originally been implanted in 1982, when Bracken first separated the joint. While the operation is not considered serious, it will necessitat considerable rehabilitation. A earlier plan called for the oper tion to be performed Monday, a lowing Bracken (6-3, 255

"Lost in a prison, can't find the key. What am I missing? Bound by steel I can't see. Breaking these chains that keep holding me down. I'm making the change and hoping I'm found."

ARTIST: KIM BRACKEN
SONGWRITER: RANDY THORDERSON

MY 1ST YEAR AT GEORGIA

TECH

turns out beyond
my wildest dreams.

As a freshman, I manage to secure
my place on the football team
and play enough to earn a varsity letter.

Playing on national television in front of crowds
of 80,000 people or more is light years away from
Las Vegas where every game
I'd scan the stands in vain
looking for my mom or Leroy.

I make the Dean's List and I'm voted in my position as an outside linebacker to the All Atlantic Coast Conference (ACC) Newcomers Team that recognizes freshmen All Stars. By the end of the football season I am in position to be a starter as a sophomore–a big deal in the ACC.

Head Coach Bill Curry calls me into his office: **"Sam, you should have a great career at Tech,** if things go well, and you don't get injured.

I see you becoming an All American and being a significant draft pick in the NFL."

Indescribable joy and hope fill my heart as Coach Curry's words sink in.

ALL MY HARD WORK IS FINALLY PAYING OFF!

GEORGIA TECH

BALL 1984

BRACKEN

After an amazing start to college and my freshman year of football–performing well in the classroom and on the field–some of my teammates who know my situation raise enough money for me to go home to Vegas during Christmas break.

I am excited and eager to return home and share all my accomplishments.

When I arrive at the airport, no one is there to greet me. Crestfallen, I use what little money I have for a cab to take me to a friend's house. For two days I search for my mother. I finally find her living in a cheap, one-bedroom motel room on the outskirts of Vegas. The room is so jammed with junk you can hardly move, and the stench is almost unbearable. Mom is obsessed with her fiancé Clayton's best friend who just got murdered. Clayton has gone to Alaska, the scene of the crime, to find out who murdered his friend.

My friend Chris DeChristo and I decide to try to bring some Christmas cheer into Mom's life. On Christmas Eve, we go to an abandoned Christmas tree lot and take a tree back to the cramped room Mom now calls home. **She sneers at my effort, and we quickly dissolve into a pattern of arguing.** I wonder why I thought it would be any different this time.

I DON'T EVER GO HOME FOR CHRISTMAS AGAIN.

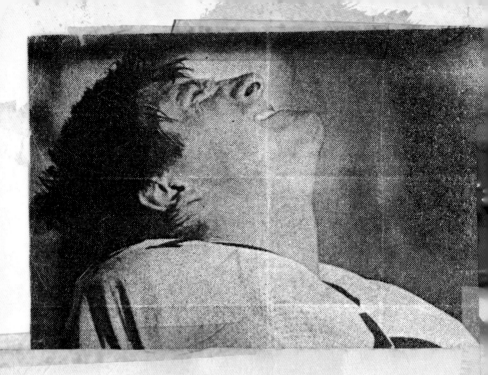

During spring football practice I am issued a pair of broken shoulder pads. Every time I make a hit, my shoulders sting. It hurts like when you hit your funny bone, but I'm definitely not laughing.

I get the shoulder pads fixed, but the pain grows worse with every hit. **Then my shoulders start coming out of their sockets on a regular basis.**

I AM IN REAL AGONY

A phone call comes from Las Vegas.

It's my first call from home since I left.

"Sam, Mom's been in a really bad car accident,

and she's in a coma," says my little brother Gerry. I go numb. His voice sounds far away. He tells me the details of how a trucker fell asleep and plowed into her…jaws of life…brain damage…arm shattered. "Come home, Sammy," he pleads.

"No, I can't come right now."

I surprise myself by how swiftly the words pop out. It's the first time in my life I've ever set a boundary with my family. I cannot explain to Gerry in that moment that I'm already on a journey. My heart tells me there is no turning back.

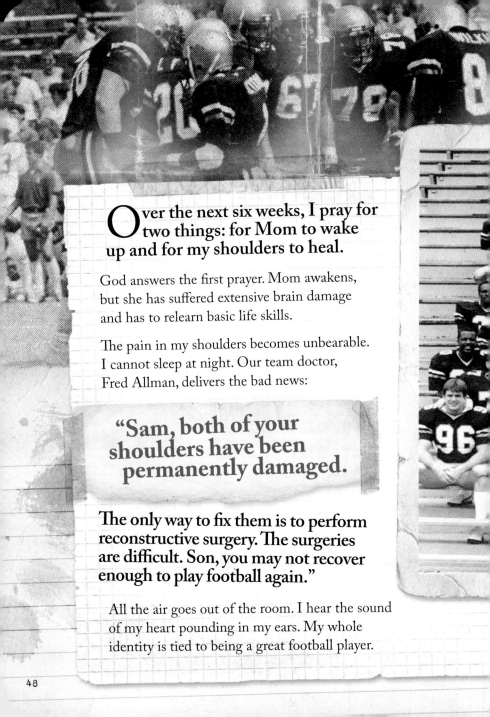

Over the next six weeks, I pray for two things: for Mom to wake up and for my shoulders to heal.

God answers the first prayer. Mom awakens, but she has suffered extensive brain damage and has to relearn basic life skills.

The pain in my shoulders becomes unbearable. I cannot sleep at night. Our team doctor, Fred Allman, delivers the bad news:

"Sam, both of your shoulders have been permanently damaged.

The only way to fix them is to perform reconstructive surgery. The surgeries are difficult. Son, you may not recover enough to play football again."

All the air goes out of the room. I hear the sound of my heart pounding in my ears. My whole identity is tied to being a great football player.

1985 Georgia Tech Varsity Football Team

DAMAGED

Q uestions swirl in my mind like a marble on a roulette wheel: **Should I have the surgery? Will I recover and play again? If I play, how will the surgeries affect my performance?**

I take the gamble and have the surgeries. The first is on my right shoulder. Dr. Allman pulls out bone chips the size of a quarter caused by my shoulders repeatedly popping out of socket. Coach Curry and Joan Conkey, now my surrogate mom whom I'd met my first Sunday at church in Atlanta, are at my bedside when I wake up. **"Don't worry about a thing, Sam," Coach Curry tells me. "You've still got your scholarship whether you play again or not."**

I cannot even bear to process what he is saying, but what does come through loud and clear is that he cares about me.

I feel comfort from Joan and Coach Curry, because their love and concern permeates the room. Alone in my hospital bed after visiting hours, I marvel at the strange feeling of knowing that someone cares for you without any obvious reason compelling their love. That feeling is raw and precious and fills my heart with hope.

My right arm and shoulder are completely immobilized for six weeks. At the end of that time, I can barely move either. They throb with the slightest movement. Next up: my left shoulder, and the process begins again. The chiseled muscle and hard-earned strength I had worked so hard to build since I was 12 years old had shriveled up. **My dream and my can-do attitude shrivel up, too.**

WHY?
WHY DID THIS
HAPPEN TO ME?

I've worked so hard to escape a life
that was like a freaked out version of
The Brady Bunch meets an episode of Cops.
Just as my dream of playing in the NFL
was starting to feel like it could happen,

MY BODY IS BROKEN.

I am depressed.
My teammates have the answer:
ROAD TRIP.

I let them talk me into it, knowing full well that their ulterior motive is to have me along as the designated driver since I don't drink. Ten of us pile into my friend Andy's van. Off we go to Destin, Florida.

Beautiful, pure white sand, the calm lapping waves and picture perfect blue sky only serve to darken my mood. We check into a motel, and all 10 of us pile into one room. I can't do much more than sit in a chair and watch while my buddies frolic in the pool with a slew of fine looking coeds.

As the day wears on, **I get more and more depressed. Self-pity engulfs me,** eroding my hope like the high tide washes away an elaborately constructed sand castle.

"My life sucks. It cannot possibly get any worse," I think glumly.

At that very moment, a flock of seagulls flies overhead and craps all over me. The smelly mess hits the top of my head, stinging my eyes and dribbles down my puny atrophied chest. **"The world has spoken: I am a crapping stick!" I scream.**

When my teammates see me, they cannot stop laughing. Finally, I start to laugh, too. **As strange as it sounds, that incident becomes a defining moment.**

I RECOGNIZE A GREAT TRUTH:

LIFE IS NOT FAIR,

but nothing good comes from sitting around feeling sorry for yourself.

God reminds me that He grants me the power to create my own destiny, regardless of how bad my circumstances appear. He's given me a beautiful gift: the gift of choice. **The course of my journey depends on the choices I make.**

I determine to do everything humanly possible to succeed and come back from the injuries.

ADVERSITY

is just a detour when you know where you're headed.

I begin the hard road to recovery with a hope that drives me to action.

Here's my self-imposed rehab schedule: **Wake up every morning at 5:30 a.m.** and go to the Student Athletic Complex Pool and swim for an hour to strengthen my shoulders. Next, climb the fence at Bobby Dodd Stadium and run the stadium stairs for at least an hour. Before most of my teammates have gotten out of bed, I have worked out for more than two hours.

After classes, I spend my afternoons in physical therapy fighting to regain the muscle mass and flexibility that I have lost. After therapy I head to the weight room. I am obsessed with getting **"strong like bull."**

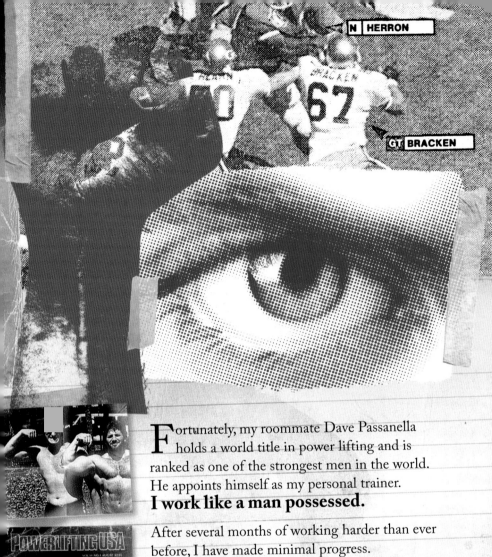

N HERRON

GT BRACKEN

Fortunately, my roommate Dave Passanella holds a world title in power lifting and is ranked as one of the strongest men in the world. He appoints himself as my personal trainer. **I work like a man possessed.**

After several months of working harder than ever before, I have made minimal progress.

Desperate, I turn once more to Coach Curry for advice. "I am working so hard, Coach. No one wants to come back more than me. What am I missing to reach my dream of being a great player?"

Coach Curry listens with concern and then says: "Son, I want you to go to the bookstore and get a binder. **In that binder make four tabs and label them spiritual, mental, physical, and emotional. Then write down a personal inventory in each section of where you are right now.** Next, take a page and write down what you want to accomplish in each section in the next year. Write down just a few things, so you won't get overwhelmed. On the next page in each section write down a compelling reason to accomplish your goals. Finally, write down how you will get it done.

Once you do that, read what you have written everyday for about 15 minutes. Then after two weeks rip out the page that described where you were.

Every day positively embrace what you want, why you want it and how you will get it.

Affirm your success in each area and keep working hard. Know that I am here for you if you need anything."

I leave that meeting with Coach Curry with the seeds of understanding that I am a whole person – with so much more to offer than my skills on the football field.

Coach Curry values me as a human being. This new understanding transforms something deep inside me.

UNDERSTANDING

THAT NOTEBOOK CHANGES EVERY

THING

SPIRITUAL   MENTAL   PHYSICAL   EMOTIONAL

I keep it in my orange duffel bag. It gives me a roadmap that helps me get clear on my destination and how to get there. I hold myself accountable to the words I write in that book. I spend 15 to 20 minutes every morning with it, gluing inspirational pictures in it and writing down great quotes. I listen to positive music and put up posters in my dorm room to remind me of the success I will soon experience.

> "You see things; and you say 'Why?' But I dream things that never were; and I say 'Why not?'" **GEORGE BERNARD SHAW**

Another year and thousands of hours of rehabilitation later, I am back. My body has changed. I have turned into a "hawg" – an offensive lineman. I weigh 285 pounds. I am stronger and more confident than ever. I re-earn a starting position and help our team win game after game, get national rankings and go to a major bowl game.

SPIRITUAL

Although I miss out on being named an All American and go undrafted by the NFL, I receive Academic All ACC honors my junior and senior years. My senior year I am nominated for the *Brian Piccolo Award* for coming back from my debilitating shoulder injuries.

I graduate from Georgia Tech with honors, with great friends and with deepened spiritual understanding through study and prayer.

I decline invitations to some professional football training camps, and I don't interview with the impressive corporations that regularly recruit on Georgia Tech's campus. Another invitation is more important to me. I pack my orange duffel bag for the next leg of my journey—serving as a full-time missionary for my church.

During my missionary service in Canada I meet the amazing woman who eventually becomes my wife. Today my beautiful wife Kim and I have three wonderful sons and a precious daughter. I'm so grateful I chose this path.

My decision to give up everything
to serve others and God
CHANGES ME FOREVER.

Ironically, the abused boy, once homeless and in special education classes, now teaches about excellence, leadership, time management and change.

The teen who feared he'd never escape Las Vegas now flies around the world for his job.

And the young man who never knew his father and whose mother abandoned him **has been blessed with his own great family.**

63

I still keep that orange duffel bag. It reminds me of where I've been and has traveled with me to places beyond my wildest dreams.

WHERE DO YOU

Maybe you don't really know. **You feel stuck in a rut.**

Maybe, like I did, **you just want to get away.** You are thinking, **"Anywhere but here."** I've been there.

Or maybe you think you've got your journey perfectly mapped out. But seemingly impassable roadblocks cause you to **crash and burn.**

The power to radically change your course and get on the path you are destined to take depends on the state you're in—your state of mind.

WANT TO GO?

SAM BRACKEN

JAPAN IMMIGRATION INSPECT
上陸許可
LANDING PERMISSIO

I am living proof
that no matter where
you are right now,

YOU CAN GET WHERE YOU WANT TO GO.

TRAVEL 151

Let me share with you
how I made this journey to radical,
lasting positive change.

These seven rules of the road

will help you find

your own true path.

"We all need
a road
that we can find
that gives us
love and peace
of mind."

RTIST: KIM BRACKEN
SONGWRITER: RANDY THORDERSON

7

DESIRE

AWARENESS

MEANING

CHOICE

LOVE

CHANGE

GRATITUDE

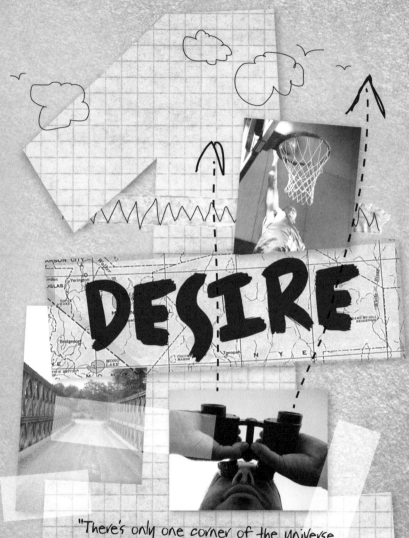

DESIRE

"There's only one corner of the universe you can be certain of improving, and that's your own self."
—ALDOUS HUXLEY

Look around.

Before you begin your journey, take a long, hard look at exactly where you are in life right now.

The desire to be different is where change begins. Change cannot happen without a **fierce desire** that burns in your heart, mind, soul and gut.

Right off the bat, let me tell you that the odds of making a lasting radical change in your life are stacked against you. Scary fact: Even when their lives are at stake, most people refuse to budge from what often proves to be the deadliest place on earth: the comfort zone.

In fact, only **one out of every nine** people acts on the **desire** for something new and different, which radically changes behavior. *Be that One!*

DESIRE

The course is set for radical change in your life when these three things collide:

1) You have a bold vision of your future;

2) You're not happy with where you are;

3) You get in touch emotionally with how your actions or inactions are negatively affecting you or someone you love.

Although I had the first two ingredients, that burning desire to change wasn't ignited until one day when I was 13 years old. Crawling in the dirt and gravel after I collapsed during track practice following a drug binge with my stepbrother, I knew I had to change. If I kept drinking and doing drugs, I had no doubt I would wind up in jail or dead.

I sure didn't like the view when I surveyed my life. It looked pretty grim.

- A crazy, messed-up home life.
- Flatlining in school.

- My role models? Mobsters, motorcycle gang members and stoners.

I wasn't sure how to be different, but I just knew I didn't want to be like THEM or MY FAMILY.

My burning desire to find a way out drove me to act differently.

 aking stock of exactly where you are can be painful, maybe even shocking. The reality of my situation was pretty heavy.

Have you ever been lost and found one of those maps with big letters that proclaim: **you are here** with an arrow marking the spot? When you are way off the mark from where you thought you were, you get that pit in your stomach. The arrow gives you a starting point, allows you to formulate a plan and start working your way out. A sense of relief washes over you.

nce you figure out where you are and how you want to be different, you must understand that **there are only two things you can control: your own thoughts and actions.** As much as I wished I had the Force like Luke Skywalker, no magical solutions or outside help materialized. The one thing I had within my power boiled down to two letters: **M-E. ME!** The desire to change sparked from my own soul. Nobody could do any of the hard work for me – **the passion had to come from inside my heart.** I had to love myself enough to change.

So what happened immediately after that day on the track? Nothing. A big fat zero. My circumstances didn't miraculously improve just because I wanted them to.

• I was still poor.

• My stepdad and Mom still got drunk, took drugs and fought like crazy.

• I was still in special education classes.

• My stepbrothers partied with my stepsisters all the time, and Lenny got in more and more trouble with the law.

In fact, my life got worse for a while. My buddies who used to come over to my house and smoke pot every day after school weren't happy with my desire for something different. My family mocked me and berated me, accusing me of thinking I was better than them.

Your circumstances won't magically change overnight. In fact, you might even find that you face more challenges.

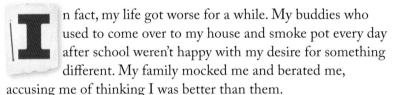

A key for me was getting new friends, different coaches, and quality mentors.

Human nature actively opposes change in the status quo. I guarantee that you will have people in your life who will want you to stay right where you are. But I eventually found a certain peace inside when I kept the promises I'd made to myself.

DESIRE

Change yourself.
Change the future.

hink about the great leaders and visionaries in our world: **Martin Luther King, Jr., Nelson Mandela, Harriet Tubman, Susan B. Anthony, Albert Einstein** and **Thomas Edison**. Did any of them make a difference without opposition?

The first two suffered imprisonment and great persecution for their beliefs. Dr. King paid the ultimate price for his, and Mandela sat in a prison cell for 27 years, because he had spearheaded the struggle against apartheid.

"The whole course of human history may depend on a change of heart in one solitary and even humble individual – for it is in the solitary mind and soul of the individual that the battle between good and evil is waged and ultimately won or lost." — M. SCOTT PECK

Tubman, who daringly helped thousands of slaves find freedom via the Underground Railroad, and Anthony, who fought against slavery and then for women's rights, put their lives on the line over and over again.

Both Einstein and Edison were thrown out of school by teachers who thought they were mentally handicapped. Throughout their careers they were intensely ridiculed for their "crazy" theories and inventions.

"Your past and your present do not determine your future."
— ANONYMOUS

What do these people have in common? Despite great pressure, they stayed true to the paths where their desires led them.

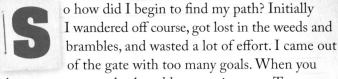

So how did I begin to find my path? Initially I wandered off course, got lost in the weeds and brambles, and wasted a lot of effort. I came out of the gate with too many goals. When you have too many goals, the odds are against you. Too many goals can be almost worse than not having any goals at all. Through trial and error, I realized that I needed to narrow my focus on a few really important goals. I also discovered that good old-fashioned hard work – hacking away daily at the mess – slowly but surely revealed the safe path beyond the tangled underbrush of my life.

Nothing of great value comes without pain, pressure and struggle. Most of us spend our lives trying to avoid any kind of suffering. But suffering eventually comes to all of us. It is the great equalizer. The only question is how you will handle the suffering and disappointment when it comes.

Don't be afraid to pinpoint your exact location on the map of your life.

You can't get where you want to go if you don't know where you are.

Ignite the flame of your **desire** for some place beyond your wildest dreams.

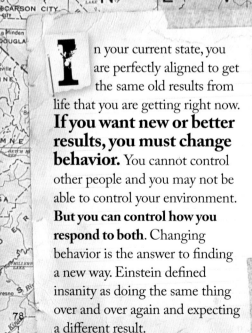

In your current state, you are perfectly aligned to get the same old results from life that you are getting right now. **If you want new or better results, you must change behavior.** You cannot control other people and you may not be able to control your environment. **But you can control how you respond to both**. Changing behavior is the answer to finding a new way. Einstein defined insanity as doing the same thing over and over again and expecting a different result.

Get a notebook like I did after my pep talk with Coach Curry, and create your own goal book. Divide it into four tabs: Emotional (HEART), Mental (MIND), Spiritual (SOUL), Physical (BODY). Take stock of exactly where you are in each area. Be honest and specific and write it all down – especially the things you want to change.

DESIRE 1

What's in your bag?

Take an inventory.
Write down exactly where you are
right now in the four key areas that
make you who you are. This exercise
will give you your starting point.

physical—body

mental—mind

spiritual—soul

emotional—heart

Here are some questions that will help you **check the contents of your bag:**

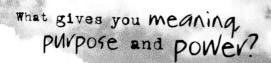

What gives you **meaning**,
purpose and **power**?

How do you want to
change your life
in each of these areas?

Why do you **want**
to be **different?**

What **motivates** you
to be different?

What goals will mean the
most to you once you've
accomplished them?

AWARENESS

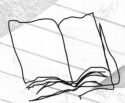

"The first step toward change is awareness.
The second step is acceptance."

— NATHANIEL BRANDEN

ADMIT ONE

151332

Find your ticket to ride.

What are you good at? Take a moment and really think about it. To get where you want to go, you've got to have a destination in mind and a **ticket to ride**.

Ignorance is the enemy of choice and change.

Knowing **what you are good at** takes self-awareness. You must know the answer to that question before you can **earn your ticket to ride** and move ahead on your journey.

So how do you find your ticket?

If you don't know where your ticket is – where your special talent resides – here are three ways you can track it down:

1) **Experience** that **A-Ha! Moment** – that divine instant when you suddenly know what your ticket is and how to get it.

2) **Listen** to someone wise who cares about you and who knows you well – a mentor, friend, family member, teacher or a coach – and ask that person to **point out** your ticket.

3) **Earn** your ticket by learning–**explore ideas through reading and examine** the lives of others you admire.

85

Claiming your ticket may not be easy.

- You may have misplaced it.
- Your ticket may not look like what you expected.
- Sometimes you lose your ticket.
- Sometimes your ticket is stamped for the wrong destination.
- Or the price of your ticket may appear too steep to pay.

Do whatever it takes to get that golden ticket.
Hold on to it. Guard it like your life depends on it.

What helped me hang onto my ticket and improve my sense of direction was developing a vision of where I wanted my journey to take me—my ultimate long-term destination.

Your vision must be clear and strong enough to inspire you to do things differently every day, every week, every month and every year.

By leveraging your ticket to ride—your talents, your attributes, your passion—your own unique vision allows you to navigate life's challenges. You can endure the worst of times and focus on your dream destination.

86

Fueled by hope and anchored in faith, a clear vision keeps you moving forward.

Very few people muster up the courage to follow their dreams in life. We listen to all the people around us who dash our hopes and call our dreams stupid. I was surrounded by people who looked no further than their next way to get high.

Growing up, most of the time I felt like this inside:

EMPTY, LONELY, WORTHLESS

Nobody in my family was cheering me on, telling me how smart I was or nurturing my potential. Identifying what I could possibly do to make myself stand out in some way was all up to me. The problem was that I walked around most days feeling like a complete loser.

My own A-Ha! Moment came that day on the track outside my junior high school. It got me thinking about what I loved. Two things popped into my mind. I loved to run and I loved to play football. I knew I probably wasn't fast enough to beat a path out of the rough area of Las Vegas where I lived.

Mike Buel Sam Mace Bracken
George Davidson

ut football was another story. I was fast for my size and big for my age. I lifted weights with a fury. Besides, football was a great coping mechanism for me. I could take some of life's frustration out on the field. And I had plenty of frustration to work out. I loved knocking the snot out of people.

As luck would have it, a movie came out that completely captured my imagination:

I sat in the darkened theater with tears stinging my eyes and rooted for Philly's underdog, Rocky Balboa.

I knew Rocky. He felt like a loser. Everybody thought he was slow. Nobody expected anything out of him. The message was loud and clear and all too familiar: **"What does it matter? He's never going to amount to anything anyway."**

But then everything shifted. The change was almost imperceptible at first, because it was a shift inside a man's soul that I saw on the movie screen. **I rooted for Rocky as he worked his heart out,** punching sides of beef and chasing chickens. He didn't worry about looking silly or what anybody else thought about his training techniques.

Rocky lined up his talent with what he loved to do. He punched his ticket to ride and fought fiercely to hang onto it. I watched that movie over and over again, savoring the moment when he ran up the steps and raised his arms in victory.

As a young teen, I decided that if I could be successful in football I could become somebody special. I initially linked my entire sense of self worth to my performance on the football field. That became my ticket to my dream destination. From eighth grade on, I poured my time and energy into becoming the best football player I could possibly be.

Later, of course, Coach Curry and other mentors helped me realize that it hurt me to have all my self worth tied to my performance on the field. Coach Curry told me that I was so much more than just a football player. **He taught me to value myself as a whole person – not just physically, but spiritually, socially and intellectually as well.**

You can be the smartest person in the world but if you can't socially interact with people and transfer knowledge or teach it, what good does smartness do? Being out of balance in any area diminishes your potential.

Hope is not a strategy. Wishful thinking didn't help me get my ticket, and it won't help you get yours. You've got to be willing to pay the price of the ticket. My mother used to always tell me that nothing in life is free – **you have to pay your own way to get where you want to go.**

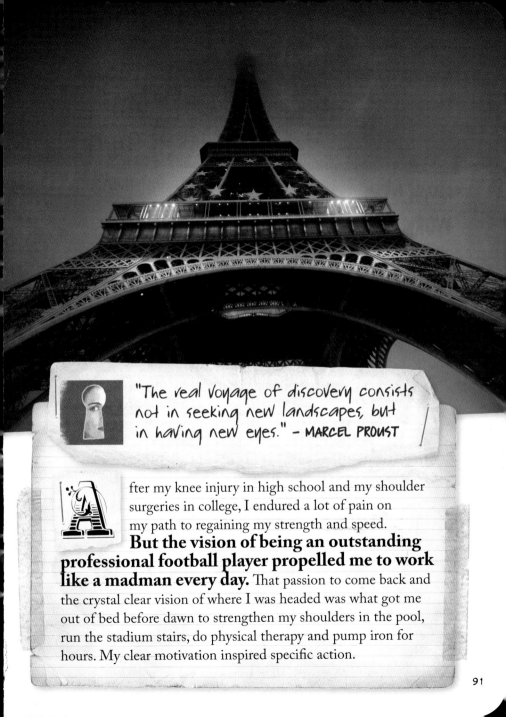

"The real voyage of discovery consists not in seeking new landscapes, but in having new eyes." — MARCEL PROUST

fter my knee injury in high school and my shoulder surgeries in college, I endured a lot of pain on my path to regaining my strength and speed. **But the vision of being an outstanding professional football player propelled me to work like a madman every day.** That passion to come back and the crystal clear vision of where I was headed was what got me out of bed before dawn to strengthen my shoulders in the pool, run the stadium stairs, do physical therapy and pump iron for hours. My clear motivation inspired specific action.

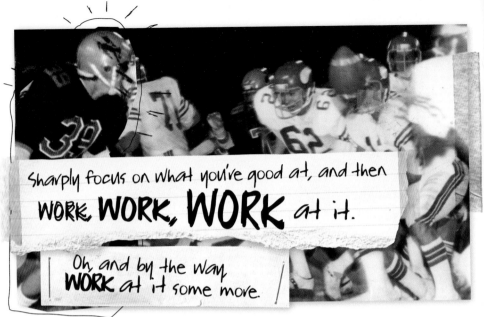

Sharply focus on what you've good at, and then
WORK, WORK, WORK at it.

Oh, and by the way
WORK at it some more.

Learn to feel the joy that comes from hard work and a job well done. Take time to savor the small victories as you make changes.

After spending time with Coach Curry, I began to understand that **getting where you want to go begins with opening your eyes and seeing yourself differently. Our potential is almost unlimited, but we hinder ourselves when we allow critics to drag us down or let low self-esteem keep us mired in a pit.**

Most companies say that their people are their most important resource, yet some don't treat them as valuable. Some coaches say that the players are what make the team, yet they abuse and berate them. My own family treated me like dirt. The crowning blow to my self-esteem came on the day my mother abandoned me when I was 15 years old. Her parting words when I walked out of our apartment with my orange duffel bag were, **"I wish you'd never been born."**

I n order to live a great life, you must learn to see yourself as a great and noble human being. For some of you, seeing yourself this way will be hard. It was difficult, nearly impossible, for me at first. I practiced having a positive mindset just like I worked out for football. In many ways, **the battle to control my own negative thoughts was harder than coming back from my football injuries. Positive self-image is critical to your ability to change.**

"If you want small changes, focus on behavior. If you want big changes, focus on your thinking." -SEAN COVEY

Creating positive affirmations and repeating them over and over again to myself helped tremendously. My wife Kim's Aunt Caroline often told her, "When you are trying to change yourself in a good way, sometimes you need to **act the part until you are the part.**" **Use affirmations, positive images, written goals and inspiring music to drown out your critics.**

Maybe the loudest, most critical voice you hear is inside your own head, a whining messenger who bleats, "You can't, you won't, you shouldn't."

"It is not the critic who counts; not the man who points out how the strong man stumbles, or where the doer of deeds could have done them better. **The credit belongs to the man who is actually in the arena,** whose face is marred by dust and sweat and blood; who strives valiantly; who errs, and comes up short again and again; because there is not effort without error and shortcoming; but who does actually strive to do the deeds; who knows the great enthusiasms, the great devotions; who spends himself in a worthy cause, who at the best knows in the end the triumphs of high achievement and who at the worst, if he fails, at least fails while daring greatness, so that his place shall never be with those cold and timid souls who know neither victory nor defeat." **—THEODORE ROOSEVELT**

A s a ninth grader, *Michael Jordan* got cut from his high school basketball team. He worked out with the team anyway and made it the next year, going on to glory as one of the *NBA's* greatest players ever.

J.K. Rowling, a single mom who struggled with thoughts of suicide and who was on public assistance, **racked up 129 rejections for *Harry Potter*.** She believed in her writing when no one else did and refused to give up her dream. Now she's richer than the Queen of England and was named *Time's 2007 Person of the Year.*

When ***Richard Branson,*** who has dyslexia, dropped out of school at age 16, **the headmaster told his mom that her son would never amount to anything.** Branson now owns more than 100 different companies including Virgin Atlantic Airways. He is deeply involved in efforts to fight world hunger and AIDS as well as global warming and was named *2007 Citizen of the Year* by the United Nations.

Each determinedly held onto their ticket and kept their dream destination in sight – no matter what the critics said. Take action on what you say your dreams are.

"The only measure of what you believe is what you do. If you want to know what people believe, don't read what they write, don't ask them what they believe, just observe what they do." — ASHLEY MONTAGU

I f you are having trouble finding your ticket – your special talent or gift – to take you to your desired destination, look to a trusted person for help. Having someone in your corner to encourage you to hang on can make all the difference. Keep in mind that your champion – the person who boosts your spirits when you feel like giving up – may come from an unexpected place.

I found my champion sweeping the floors of the athletic gear store that my stepuncle owned. His name was Brian Cross. Because he was so grossly overweight and out of shape, I was shocked when he told me he'd played college football.

96

Turns out he had been a high school All American as a tight end and earned a college scholarship. He had offers from major schools all over the country, but had to settle for a small, third-tier school in Kentucky due to his poor grades in high school.

"Still as a college freshman, **I was getting letters from NFL teams like the Oakland Raiders and the San Diego Chargers,"** he told me one day as we shot hoops at the YMCA. **"Then I fell in with the wrong crowd, flunked out of school and eventually wound up in Las Vegas."**

Once I shared with him my dream to play college football, he became my mentor. He showed up faithfully every Sunday afternoon to pick me up from wherever I was staying. He'd spend his day off passing me the football, working on drills and teaching me all he knew about the game we both loved. **He also planted a seed when he shared with me about his spiritual beliefs and how they had helped him get off the wrong path.**

During my junior and senior years in high school I never came out of a football game. I played both ways and on special teams. Brian became a fixture in the stands. **I was named All Conference and All State as a defensive end.**

I'm grateful to Brian Cross because he made himself vulnerable and showed me what could happen if I lost my ticket and my way. He was my champion, cheering me on.

Silence the critics, including the one in your own head. **Write one sentence that sums up your special gift and repeat it to yourself as often as needed.** For example, mine was:

"I am a great football player."

Now it has become: "I am a prolific author, speaker and producer committed to positively impacting the lives of millions."

I f you're having trouble identifying your special gift, find a champion and enlist that person's help. Write down your champion's name.

Create a vision of the dream destination to which your ticket will take you.

This long-term or lifetime goal gives you the answer to the **BIG WHAT – what your journey is all about.**

Your vision is an emotional picture of your desired destination. It should leverage your ticket to ride. Explore your interests, talents, and strengths.

Your vision should be so emotional and so powerful that it ignites your soul and causes you to do things differently every day, week, month, and year.

Write down your vision and express it in such a way that it unlocks your passion to change and moves you to positive action every day.

P.S. Keep it simple.

The Big "What"
What's your
dream destination?

Find your *ticket to ride.*

What are you *good* at?

What will
your ticket

Are you willing
to pay the price?

cost you?

Here are some questions
to help you determine your Vision:

What will your life's great
and unique contribution be?

What are you
passionate about?

At the end of your life
what will people say about you?

MEANING

"It is in changing that we find purpose."

—HERACLEITUS OF EPHESUS

Check your compass.

You know where you want to go and you've got your ticket to ride. Now you've got to learn to check your compass for guidance.

I believe that each of us is born with a light that helps us know the difference between right and wrong. This internal compass–our conscience–ideally points us in the right direction. Sometimes this light grows dim. The compass no longer shows true north, and it stops directing us. **Nothing is scarier than being hopelessly lost, aimlessly wandering without a sense of direction.**

In our hurry-up, pressure-filled world, it's easy to get out of sync with your own internal compass–**that voice inside you that lets you know when you're off track,** or, in my case, hurtling in the wrong direction. Take time daily to listen to your own inner voice.

My compass was spinning wildly out of control.

learned to read from pornography magazines that my stepdad, Leroy, left lying around our apartment. I thought it was normal for a dad to punch his son square in the face.

And how many 12-year-olds do you know who share drugs with their moms?

My hardwiring was seriously haywire, and my compass was broken.

Because of my chaotic home life, I missed out on a lot of the basic life skills people normally learn from their families. For example, when I arrived at Georgia Tech I had 17 cavities. **I didn't know that most people brush their teeth at least two times a day and I had no idea what flossing was.** These skills were simply not in my realm of experience.

I often felt out of sync with the norm. To get going in the right direction, I had to be anchored by what is right.

No matter what your current environment, you can learn to use your internal compass.

Mine had to be **recalibrated** before I could trust it to point me in the right direction.

"Whatever is true, whatever is noble, whatever is right, whatever is pure, whatever is lovely, whatever is admirable — if anything is excellent or praiseworthy — think about such things."
— PHILIPPIANS 4:8

s a teenager, **I tuned into my internal compass by filling myself up with good things.** I listened to **uplifting music** and watched **inspiring movies.** I wrote down **positive affirmations** in my notebook. I plastered posters with **motivational messages** on the walls of wherever I was staying. I read **compelling books and other spiritual writings.** Through work, school and church, I sought out successful friends and their families and asked if I could hang out with them. Most importantly, I studied the Bible and other inspiring writings daily and applied true principles to my life.

MEANING

Do whatever it takes to protect your mind and your heart from negativity. Fill yourself up with light every day.

o this day, I make it a habit to fill myself up with the good on a daily basis to help me stay the course. The important tools I use to set my internal compass involve three things: **what I think about**

1) my long view 2) my values 3) my purpose.

What you value in this life is revealing.

When I decided to radically change the course of my life as a teenager, **I discovered that I felt so much better inside when I tried to be kind, friendly and good.** I wrote down that I wanted to become a nice person, someone kind whom others could count as a friend. That probably sounds pretty basic, but from where I was at that point in my life – surrounded by mobsters, drug dealers and motorcycle gang members – that was a bold step. I didn't know it then, but I was committing to a new value. In my household, what was valued was being tough. That meant fighting to get whatever you wanted, even if somebody got hurt in the process.

"Be the change you want
to see in the world." -GANDHI

Lying, cheating, stealing and being cruel to people brought me misery. **I learned that if I helped people, loved them, and made them laugh, my actions made me feel better inside.** I felt so much better being kind that it helped me change.

All through high school, I kept that thought – be a kind person – in my mind. **I wanted desperately to be the opposite of what I saw at home.** Recently at my twentieth year high school class reunion, I was delighted to learn that I was remembered as the jock who was smart and who was kind to everyone.

What's important to you? Would an outsider looking at your life be able to tell what your **core values** are by how you act and how you spend your time? Whether you recognize it or not, you live what you believe. **Actions really do speak louder than words.**

Your purpose or mission is
what makes life meaningful.

**Without a purpose, we drift and
lose hope. There is tremendous
power in finding your purpose.**
Courageous Holocaust survivor **Viktor E. Frankl**
devoted his time in the concentration camps
to preventing other prisoners' suicides by
encouraging them not to give up.

In Frankl's powerful and influential book, *Man's Search For Meaning*, which chronicles his experiences in four different camps including Auschwitz, the neurologist and psychiatrist noted a commonality among the survivors: **their ability to find a sense of purpose.** They found a reason to go on, no matter how dire their circumstances and how intense their suffering.

When you suffer, you have two choices:

ONE: You can **become bitter,** which eventually consumes you and leads to more pain and suffering.

 TWO: You can gain empathy for others' pain through your own suffering.

Empathy is one of God's great gifts to us and gives us the opportunity to use our experiences to comfort other people going through similar hardships.

Even in the midst of terrible suffering, you can find purpose

y purpose is to help people unlock their ability to make positive changes. I could have allowed all that I suffered to make me **bitter** – or I could choose to let it make me a **better** person.

I recognize that my suffering doesn't compare with some of the horrors to which millions of human beings have been subjected. However, my suffering led me to have great compassion and empathy for people in tough situations. My experiences shaped me: as a poor kid who grew up in a violent and abusive household; as a college football player who fought to come back from injuries; then as a missionary who had to learn how to really love all people from all different backgrounds. Had I been given a choice, I don't know that I would have selected this sometimes painful path. But today **I wouldn't trade my journey for anything. It defines who I am and compels me to share my story in order to reach out to others.**

Bitter or better? Sounds simple, but it's a hard-fought choice that each of us is called upon to make. On your journey, you will encounter circumstances that are difficult. Maybe you're on a road of sorrow right now. No matter the road you're on, the difference that one vowel makes between the "b" and the "t" will determine your future steps. Make the "I" an "E."

Finding meaning in our suffering, experiences and struggles can bring a great deal of joy into our lives. It also helps us on our journey to change. When you understand the purpose that drives you on your journey, it also helps you say "no" to the things that aren't going to bring you closer to your destination.

"It's easy to say 'no!' when there's a deeper 'yes!' burning inside." —STEPHEN R. COVEY

Make sure your compass is aligned with your vision, values and purpose. **Your purpose gives you the answer to the BIG WHY behind your long view and your goals.** What are the values or rules that guide your journey? **The principles that you choose to live by define you as a human being.** Solid values allow you to trust your internal compass and help you stay on course.

Write down what you currently value or want to value and what the benefit of each value is.

Use photos, sayings, art and words that are meaningful to you, and make a collage on a sheet of paper or poster board to illustrate what you value. Be creative. Think about your values in all four areas of your life. Keep your collage where you can see it, so that it reminds you to stay true to your path.

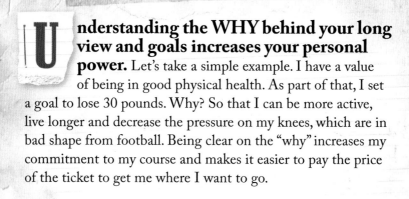

Understanding the WHY behind your long view and goals increases your personal power. Let's take a simple example. I have a value of being in good physical health. As part of that, I set a goal to lose 30 pounds. Why? So that I can be more active, live longer and decrease the pressure on my knees, which are in bad shape from football. Being clear on the "why" increases my commitment to my course and makes it easier to pay the price of the ticket to get me where I want to go.

What's your purpose?

Why are you on this journey?
Write down what you are good at and why.
Now connect to the reasons
behind your actions.

Imagine compelling reasons
for you to do things differently.

What gives your life
meaning?

What makes you feel
fulfilled?

Name 10 things that
come *easily* for you.

Name 10 people whom
you admire and what you
admire about them.

If your house caught fire,
what **3 things** would you grab?

If you won $1 million,
what would you do with
the money?

What keeps showing up?
Look for the *commonalities.*

What is the *reason*
behind your dream?

How is your *passion*
reflected in this dream?

How do you want

to make an *impact?*

Contemplate your
long view.

CHOICE

EXIT

"I can't change the direction of the wind, but I can adjust my sails to always reach my destination." — JIMMY DEAN

ENTER

Pick your path and pack your bag.

Now that you know where you want to go and you have your ticket to ride, how do you get there from here?

You must pick your path with your end destination in mind.

As a high school freshman, I set a goal of becoming a pro football player and an attorney. Okay, I admit it: I chose the latter career, because from what I'd seen on television, attorneys lived in nice houses and wore nice suits. To a poor kid with few role models, being an attorney appeared to offer a nice life. In order to reach those goals, I had to pick a path that would get me where I wanted to go.

To snag a scholarship, I knew I had to turn in consistently stellar performances on the football field, as well as study hard and make good grades throughout high school. And I didn't want to play football just anywhere. I wanted to play for a Division 1 school, so that I'd stand a good chance of making it into the pros. I also decided that just going to college wasn't enough. It had to be a school that was well-respected academically so that I'd stand the best chance of getting into law school. That was the path that I thought offered the clearest route out of the life of poverty I was living.

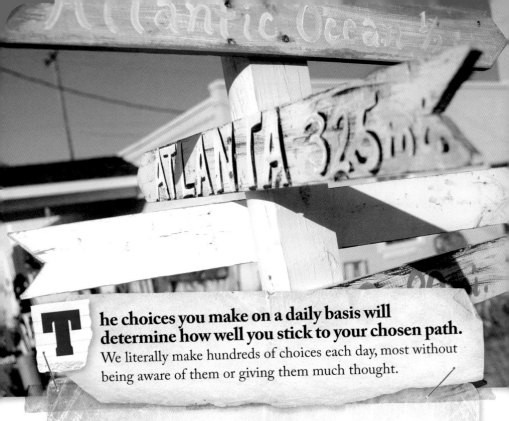

The choices you make on a daily basis will determine how well you stick to your chosen path. We literally make hundreds of choices each day, most without being aware of them or giving them much thought.

I HAD TO CHOOSE:

to be disciplined and focus on my homework even though there was often chaos going on around me;

to ignore the temptation to take drugs or drink in order to numb myself to the pain of my life;

to be dedicated to grueling, time-consuming workouts even though I was exhausted by working as a busboy to support myself, going to school, playing ball and running track;

to keep on hoping even when my knee got hurt when I was prepping for the All-Star game in Las Vegas the summer after my senior year in high school.

aking those choices didn't come easy to me. Free will – the ability to make choices – is hardwired into all of us. It's at the core of our being. But we get tangled in our thinking and impaired in our ability to make good choices when we aren't allowed to exercise our free will in a safe, healthy environment.

I was surrounded by adults who were mobsters and motorcycle gang members. My stepbrother regularly tortured me physically, and my stepfather randomly beat me. My mom was overwhelmed with trying to keep us all afloat, so she failed to protect me.

When you don't have good boundaries, the temptation to think of yourself as a victim without choices becomes stronger and stronger.

Failing to recognize that you have choices leads you to resign yourself to your current position in life.

The danger sign is feeling helpless or having despair.

Don't allow yourself to be the victim, villain or martyr. Maybe your boss failed to recognize your talent and gave the promotion you think you deserved to someone else. Maybe your dad drank all the rent money and your family got evicted yet again. Maybe a health crisis forced you to declare bankruptcy. Maybe an insurance company denied a legitimate claim that sent you into a financial tailspin. A lot of situations don't measure up to our notion of fair play.

can promise you one thing: **making the wrong choices, being paralyzed by fear or refusing to make a choice at all will get you nowhere.**

> By refusing to make a choice, you make a choice.

> That's a place you don't want to be.

What helped me stay the course, despite all the obstacles, temptations and frustrations? **I kept my end goal in mind.** I imagined myself on a podium, accepting an award for my play in college. I heard my name called during the NFL draft. I envisioned being in a courtroom, arguing a case persuasively in front of a jury. I dreamed of one day having the financial stability to support a happy family of my own.

Ignorance is the enemy of choice. Once you have the desire to change and the awareness of what you want to accomplish, choice springs up around you.

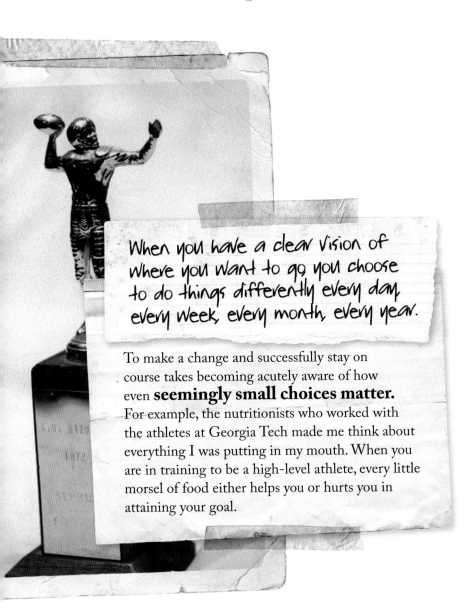

When you have a clear vision of where you want to go you choose to do things differently every day, every week, every month, every year.

To make a change and successfully stay on course takes becoming acutely aware of how even **seemingly small choices matter.** For example, the nutritionists who worked with the athletes at Georgia Tech made me think about everything I was putting in my mouth. When you are in training to be a high-level athlete, every little morsel of food either helps you or hurts you in attaining your goal.

When I was a junior, the nutritionists determined that we should no longer gorge ourselves on red meat for the three days leading up to a game. Red meat proved too hard to digest and diverted much-needed energy during the game. Instead, they encouraged us to carbo-load in order to improve our fourth quarter performance. **Of course, ultimately we had a choice of following the new advice or not.** I did and found that a simple change in my diet made a world of difference in keeping up my energy level throughout the crucial fourth quarter. That experience changed the way I looked at food. I came to see it as fuel.

A seemingly inconsequential choice can make a big difference in your life.

Don't underestimate its importance.

Think about a pilot. When he or she puts together a flight plan, the pilot knows the final destination. Yet in the course of getting there, the pilot is typically off the flight plan about 90 percent of the flight. The pilot constantly makes small adjustments and choices to safely get to the end point.

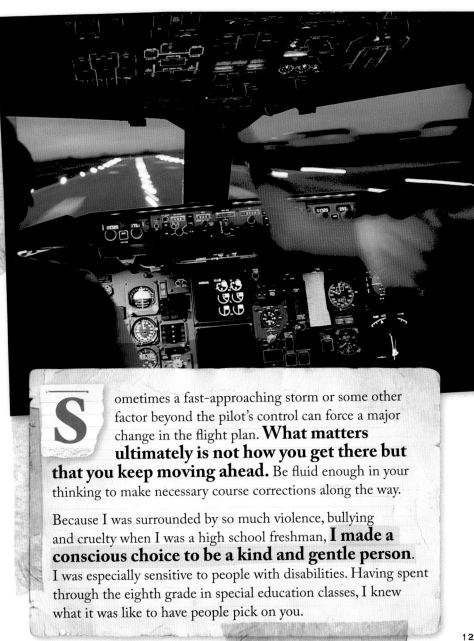

Sometimes a fast-approaching storm or some other factor beyond the pilot's control can force a major change in the flight plan. **What matters ultimately is not how you get there but that you keep moving ahead.** Be fluid enough in your thinking to make necessary course corrections along the way.

Because I was surrounded by so much violence, bullying and cruelty when I was a high school freshman, **I made a conscious choice to be a kind and gentle person.** I was especially sensitive to people with disabilities. Having spent through the eighth grade in special education classes, I knew what it was like to have people pick on you.

uring my junior year at Georgia Tech, one of my friends, Bruce Wheeler, was in a terrible car accident on Christmas Eve. He suffered a severe brain injury. A senior with a 3.2 grade point average, Bruce was the kind of bigger-than-life guy whom everybody loved. He was brilliant, funny, handsome – and he came from a loving, old money Atlanta family. President of the Ramblin' Wreck Club and treasurer of Sigma Nu Fraternity, he was an active member of both the ANAK Society and the Order of Omega, the Greek honor society. Everything seemed to be falling in place for Bruce. The wreck changed all of that in a split second.

Bruce wasn't expected to survive, but after several months in a coma, he woke up and started the process of rebuilding his life. He had to relearn to walk, talk and feed himself. After much rehabilitation, he returned to school at Georgia Tech. However, he needed a lot of assistance with basic life skills.

My heart went out to Bruce.

My mother had suffered a brain injury, too, when she was hit by a Mack truck during my sophomore year in college. I understood a little bit of what Bruce was dealing with. I invited him to parties, helped him with his wheelchair and books and remained his friend.

That wasn't the case with some people. What had once been a wide circle of friends for Bruce grew small. It's funny how tragedy can make some people run as if they fear it might be contagious.

After much hard work, Bruce got his degree and graduated. At graduation, he gamely struggled out of his wheelchair and walked across the stage using a cane to get his diploma for his degree in management.

During my senior year I was nominated for the **ANAK Society,** an honor bestowed annually on about a dozen seniors. To be considered for what is the highest honor at Georgia Tech, you must be nominated by a member and deemed excellent in all four areas of the whole-person philosophy that **Coach Curry** emphasized with me: intellectually, socially, physically and spiritually. To my amazement, **I was selected and inducted into the ANAK Society.** For years, I wondered who had put me up for that honor.

ANAK
FOUNDED IN 1908

Georgia Institute of Technology
Atlanta, Georgia

May 7, 1986

Dear Samuel Ray Bracken,

Georgia Tech fosters many who in some capacity are leaders. However, few is the number who can be singled out as "Giants among men". Few indeed have been given the rare combination of leadership, personal worth, and character that merits them the universal respect and esteem of their peers.

Samuel Ray Bracken, we of the ANAK Society believe you to b a person who shares with each of us an abiding love for Georgia Tech. We know you to be one who, through your leadership and personal achievements, has been of great service to Georgia Tech a person who possesses a genuinely exceptional personality - one which is characterized by a spiritual depth, one which has the highest regard for our fellow man.

n the course of writing this book, my co-author and I took our oldest sons to a Georgia Tech football game. In the parking lot, we happened to run into Bruce and his parents. I was thrilled to see my old friend who was just as upbeat as I remembered. Then Bruce solved a mystery for me. **He mentioned that he was the one who had nominated me.** *"You were still my friend and made time for me after the accident,"* he said, the words coming slowly and with great difficulty.

Tears sprang to my eyes. I hugged Bruce again.

As a high school freshman my simple decision to be kind to everybody I came into contact with – especially people that others overlooked or found difficult to love – **had brought me an honor beyond any I could have dreamed about.**

Bruce is truly a hero.
Despite severe pain and disabilities, he has **tirelessly lobbied** Congress, several Presidents and others in power to expand the rights of people with disabilities. He started a non-profit organization called Head Injured Pals, Inc., to encourage others who have suffered head injuries and their families. He chose to move forward on a new path even after his life got rearranged in a way that would have crushed the spirit of many others.

"Don't worry about what you can't do; do what you can do," Bruce likes to say. That's solid advice.

The more you exercise your right to choose – even in the small things and especially when you've been fooled into believing you don't have a choice – **the more likely you are to make the right choice when it counts.**

Think of your right to choose as a muscle and give it a workout on a daily basis. God promises us that no matter how tempted we may be to feel hopeless in a situation, He always provides a way out.

"No temptation has seized you except what is common to man. And God is faithful; He will not let you be tempted beyond what you can bear. But when you are tempted, He will also provide a way out so that you can stand up under it." – 1 CORINTHIANS 10:12-14

During our lives we all experience defining moments.

These are the big forks in the road when we choose to act or react to our circumstances. How we see things affects our behavior, and our behavior is what affects our results in life. Sometimes choice means choosing to see your situation in a different light.

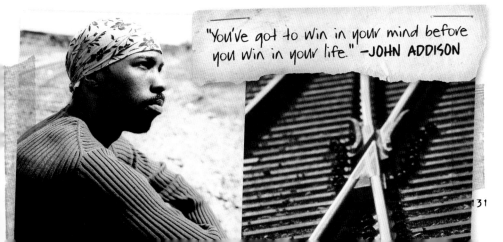

"You've got to win in your mind before you win in your life." –JOHN ADDISON

good friend pointed out that fact to me one day after I related the story of my mother kicking me out when I was 15 years old. At that time, I thought that my life couldn't get any worse. **My own mother rejected me, screaming at me that she wished I'd never been born. Strangely, in the middle of her rant, she suddenly said,**

"Someday you'll look back on this day and thank me."

My friend said, *"You know your mom was right. Because she kicked you out, you ended up living in a normal household for the first time in your life. You saw what a loving family could be like. If you had kept living with your mom, you might never have found the path you were meant to take. **Your mom's abandonment turned out to be a tremendous blessing.**"*

I was stunned to hear him say those words in relation to such a painful moment in my life. But the more I thought about it, the more I realized that he was absolutely right.

Bad things happen to good people every day.

Ask yourself one tough question whenever you experience a tragedy or hardship: **What good can come out of this situation?** Forcing yourself to answer that question will help you make the choices that will get you to that better place faster.

The power of choice means never having to be a victim.

Just switching out a few letters at the end transforms the word "Victim" into "Victorious." Use the power of choice to make that transformation.

One of my defining moments came on that track when I was 13 years old and decided to stop doing drugs and drinking.

Yet another defining moment came when the flock of seagulls made their deposits all over me as I sat by the pool in Destin, Florida, feeling sorry for myself after my second shoulder surgery. I recognized that I could either get back on the path to my dream of being a professional football player, or I could remain mired in a sinkhole of self-pity. I chose the route that eventually helped me regain a starting position on the Georgia Tech team that put together the school's best record in 20 years.

A major defining moment for me was when I chose an entirely new path once I graduated from Tech. I replaced my dream of playing professional football with my desire to serve God as a full-time missionary.

Sometimes our sense of direction when we are faced with a big decision is stellar, and that inner compass guides us to the right path. Other times the route we choose ends up not being the best way to get where we want to go. We wind up stuck in a ditch or lost in the woods.

When we understand our unique purpose and keep our eyes focused on our dream destination – **that vision of what we clearly want out of life – picking the right path becomes easier.** Your vision may require you to have the courage to blaze a new trail.

That's what happened to me. I wasn't following in the footsteps of any role model when I started on my journey to play pro football. My vision caused me to follow a path into uncharted territory.

I'd only been on a plane one other time in my life before I came to Georgia Tech. Nobody—except my mom—in my family had even tried to go to college much less been awarded a scholarship. I'd never been to the South. **I could have allowed the major roadblock that stops so many people to stop me as well.**

That roadblock is fear of the unknown. And that roadblock often sends people racing back to what I've come to think of as Deadman's Curve: **the comfort zone.**

That place is a dreamkiller.

I worked hard throughout high school to earn a full-ride football scholarship, knowing that was my only chance to go to school. Offers flooded in from many of the top football schools in the nation, but I turned them all down. I had my heart set on playing for Brigham Young University, which had a fantastic football program at the time and held the promise of a wholesome environment. **I was thrilled when I was promised a scholarship.**

Then, shortly before graduation and right after my stepdad Leroy died of cancer, I learned that my scholarship had gone to someone else. I'd be lying if I told you I bounced right back from that crushing blow. **But I chose to stay focused on my goal: to play college ball at a football powerhouse that was also academically challenging.** I decided that I would attend BYU on an academic scholarship and walk on.

spent all summer working out with BYU's team and working to build the stadium in order to earn money for school. Then my knee was injured during a practice leading up to the All-Star game that I'd returned to Las Vegas to play in. Once again, my plans were shattered.

At that point, I veered off course. Working at the casinos, you can make pretty good money hustling tips, and some girls from my high school made close to $100,000 a year dancing topless in a show called *Spice on Ice*. I'd been accepted to the University of Nevada at Las Vegas. I rationalized and decided that I could go to school and work at one of the casinos. I knew the terrain. I was tired of struggling to find my way out.

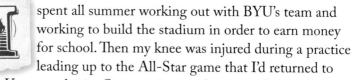

Lucky for me, I stopped and asked for directions.

After my knee injury, Dr. Andrew Welch, the orthopedic surgeon I saw, and Dave Denham, my physical therapist, took an interest in me. **Dr. Welch helped me remember the promise I'd made to myself and the lofty goals I'd set.** He gently pointed out that I was about to make a bad choice and go down the path that looked the easiest.

Those two men showed me a path that would get me back on the route to my dream of playing football and provide me with a degree in a field that interested me (At the time, UNLV was only accredited for a degree in hospitality/hotel management). Dr. Welch and Dave helped me put together a marketing package with a reel of my best high school films and a cover letter highlighting my accomplishments. We sent those packages to 25 excellent schools with strong football and academic programs. Ten contacted me. Five showed interest, but only Georgia Tech extended an invitation that led to a scholarship. **All I needed was that one clear path, and Georgia Tech gave me that path.**

ew people make it to their destination via a straight shot. You'll likely encounter detours, potholes and road hazards along the way. **On the surface, my promised scholarship that was given away to someone else plus my knee injury seemed like complete and utter disasters.** If those two events hadn't happened, I never would have landed at Georgia Tech and met Coach Curry or Joan and Don Conkey, all of whom became surrogate parents to me. And because Georgia Tech emphasized the importance of the whole person and being well-rounded, I was empowered to let go of the negative baggage that was weighing me down.

Hope is a muscle. I chose to exercise that muscle and have faith that I had good directions. I hurdled the road block of fear.

The other big choice you face before you embark on your grand adventure is **what to pack**. The smart traveler knows to bring as little as possible but all the right stuff. Most of us tend to pack too much stuff.

Extra baggage weighs you down and adds unnecessary stress. **Ditch the excess baggage.**

When I packed **my orange duffel bag** and left Las Vegas behind, I traveled light. I made a decision to let go of the past. I focused on the road ahead. Dwelling in the no-man's land of the past often leads to regrets and sadness. It can completely derail you. Besides, you can be so busy looking back that you miss the beautiful scenery spread before you. **I didn't want to miss any of the magnificent vistas my new future promised.**

I forgave my mother for abandoning me

Forgiving others and yourself is a vital part of change. Get rid of the excess baggage. Destiny delivered the chance to decide whether to let go of any hatred toward my biological father. Shortly after my mother kicked me out, she revealed that when she was stationed with the Army in Mississippi during the Cuban Missile Crisis **a superior officer date-raped her.** When she confronted him with her pregnancy, he denied that I was his. My mother got an honorable discharge and went home to Oregon in disgrace.

om told me his name and that he'd gone on to be a judge and lived in Florida. During one of our road trips to Florida with my teammates, we wound up in the town where my mom said he lived. That night at a party, I was chatting with a girl and mentioned that I knew someone in town and gave the man's name. *"That's my best friend's dad,"* she said smiling. *"How cool is that?"*

Before I could choke out a response, she scrawled the home phone number on a scrap of paper and gave it to me. I headed back to the hotel, clutching the number. **I'd dreamed of finding my biological father,** but now, sitting on the polyester bedspread and looking at the phone, I wasn't so sure. I got down on my knees and prayed. Then I dialed the number with trembling hands.

I hung up, never making a connection.

"If you judge people, you have no time to love them." - MOTHER TERESA

hy didn't I complete the call? Because my faith demands that I forgive. In that flash, I decided that it was unlikely that anything good could come of my sudden appearance in that man's life. The knowledge of my existence would likely bring a good deal of pain for him and his family. When I balanced out my desire to know him against the possible damage my phone call would cause, I decided to let it go.

When I got up off my knees, I felt light. There's a beautiful freedom in forgiveness. Travel light, travel right.

Anger, bitterness, hatred – all are heavy loads to carry. Emotional baggage is the primary thing that slows us down on the path we're intended to take.

Sometimes we need to shed relationships, because they are hurtful and keep us from growing. In my case, I had to separate from my family for a while. I still loved my mom, Gerry and my other siblings, but I couldn't really move ahead while I was emotionally embroiled in my old life. For me, literally having thousands of miles between us helped me start to understand my true potential.

You may not need to physically remove yourself from a relationship, or you may not be able to for some reason. But there's a way of minimizing another person's impact on your emotional health. Think about each of your closest relationships. **Is that person helping you along your path or is he or she holding**

you back? If someone close to you is a negative influence, choose to minimize their importance in your life. Whenever the person who drags you down starts talking, practice seeing them in your mind as this tiny being – the size of a housefly. It's a funny visual, but that exercise will gradually help you to steel yourself against the onslaught of negativity.

For a flight, if your bags are too heavy, you **pay a penalty.** Lugging around heavy baggage slows you down on your journey and makes you miss the beauty and joy of travel, because you're focused on your burden. Sometimes hauling too much stuff with you causes you to miss your connection entirely. **Heavy baggage wears you out.** What you choose to leave behind – bad habits, negative thoughts, emotional vampires who suck the life out of you – can be just as important as what you pack.

Pick your path and pack wisely.

For each goal, I write down specific, actionable steps that I track on a daily, weekly and monthly basis. I've found that the degree of my success in achieving my goals directly correlates to how detailed I am about the steps I plan to take toward each goal. I keep the big goals and the gaps on a bookmark that I can look at every day.

What's in your bag?

Experienced travelers rely on a packing list. What will you need on your journey and when you arrive at your destination? Although all my orange duffel bag had in it when I arrived at Georgia Tech was a few T-shirts, some underwear and an extra pair of jeans, I had learned by that point to pack my bag with some important items, metaphorically speaking.

What threatens to block your chosen path or slow you down? Prepare for a successful journey by anticipating possible problems and thinking through solutions. For example, after getting a 2.7 GPA my first semester at Georgia Tech, I realized that I needed extra help academically. I found out that through the athletic department's total person program, I was eligible for free tutoring. After that I never missed a tutoring session in vital classes, and I graduated with honors.

What gaps do you need to close for each goal?

(P.S. If there's no gap, there's no goal.) For example, here are my current goals and how I intend to close the gap:

physical BODY

- **SAM'S GOAL:** Lose weight – Go from 325 to 275 pounds in six months.
- **CLOSE THE GAP** with diet and exercise.

mental MIND

- **SAM'S GOAL:** Become a successful author and speaker.
- **CLOSE THE GAP** with the production and market launch of *My Orange Duffel Bag: A Journey to Radical Change* and sell my first 100,000 copies by the end of the year.

emotional HEART

- **SAM'S GOAL:** Continue to deepen my relationship with Kim and our children.
- **CLOSE THE GAP** by spending quality time with Kim and by helping my kids feel secure and each reach his/her potential.

spiritual SOUL

- **SAM'S GOAL:** Get closer to God and do His will in all things.
- **CLOSE THE GAP** with regular prayer, scripture study, fasting and service.

Here are some of the things I take with me on my journey:

Because my self-esteem was pretty much non-existent, **I needed encouragement from books that contained uplifting messages.** So I constantly read books that fed my brain and helped me in one of those four areas. I'm still a voracious reader. On flights I always take a book that will expand my horizons and help me in one of the four key areas of my development, and I listen to audio books on my iPod in my car.

Music lifts my mood so I always carry favorites with me and listen to them. I need a soundtrack to my life. We've also produced some great music for *My Orange Duffel Bag* that features music written by Randy Thorderson and performed by my wife Kim Bracken and Echo's brother singer/songwriter Kevin Montgomery.

Every year I create a goal book so that I can track my progress in all four areas. I use it to journal my thoughts about my progress, any roadblocks I encounter and the victories along the way. I've always kept it in my orange duffel bag.

Positive affirmations can help us stay on the right path. Our minds are amazing. If I'm struggling with negative thoughts, I find sayings, scriptures and encouraging quotes that address my issues. I write them on index cards and memorize them, replacing my garbage thinking with positives that help me along my journey.

I **keep mementos that remind me of how far I've come.** One of my treasures is a letter from my mom that she wrote to me when I was on the missionary field. In it she praised me for my creativity and encouraged me to explore that side of myself. Another is a letter that Coach Curry wrote to me in response to a letter I'd written to him in which I questioned my decision to forego a pro football career in order to serve as a missionary. In his reply, he told me that I was a bigger winner in his eyes, because of my convictions. I still weep when I think of the tenderness of his words.

Once you've made substantial progress along your path, reflecting upon how far you've come can be sweet.

TRAVEL TIP

151332

What you choose to pack should be tools and strategies you need to reach your dream destination. Note beside each item on your packing list how it will aid you on your journey.

What are
your goals?

What do you want to accomplish in the next 12 months in the four areas that help you to be **a well-balanced person?**

Mentally

Physically

Spirituelly

Emotionally

149

What's in
your
bag?

LOVE

"Love is a choice you make from moment to moment." - BARBARA DE ANGELIS

LOVE

Choose your traveling companions and guides carefully.

A big part of what makes a journey memorable is who you choose as your tour guide, who you share your adventure with and how you interact with the people you meet along the way.

Choosing the right people to accompany you on your adventure can make it more fun. And the right guide might know a shortcut, direct you to the right path or steer you on a wonderful side trip that you would miss if you continued on all by your lonesome.

Conversely, traveling with someone who has a **completely different purpose from you can be a real drag.** The wrong traveling companion can impede your progress and get you way off track.

A lot of people make this mistake. They surround themselves with people who don't support the positive changes they want to make. These toxic people are emotional vampires who poison the environment for change. They suck the life out of your goals and dreams.

"No person is your friend who demands your silence, or denies your right to grow." – ALICE WALKER

f course, we don't always have control over who is in our lives. I had no choice about what family I was born into. **Sometimes you have bad coaches, difficult bosses, mean classmates or grumbling coworkers.** When an authority figure in your life is negative, actively seek out positive people to help minimize the harm these toxic bullies cause.

Surround yourself with positive, powerful people. You'll be amazed at how much you'll be elevated and supercharged.

soar

In other words, hang out with eagles and you'll soar. Hang out with pigs and you'll stink

fter my mom threw me out, I stayed with the families of friends from school and church. **I started to discover how normal families live.** I consciously hung out with the kids who were good students and who had good morals.

Coming from a place where I suffered random beatings, mental and verbal abuse, sexual degradation and emotional neglect, I had a lot to learn about navigating a path to peace and joy.

I also had to make a decision. Would I allow anybody to be part of my journey? Given my background I had every excuse not to trust people. However, I decided to actively look for the good in people on a daily basis and go after healthy relationships. I made the choice to be open and to love. This choice put me in a vulnerable place, but I had to go there in order to get where I wanted to go.

To love and be loved is one of our greatest needs.

- Love can propel us far along our chosen path.
- Love opens the door to forgiveness and helps you get rid of extra baggage.
- Love is powerful. It breaks down barriers.
- Love fills our souls with gratitude.
- Love means looking for the good in everyone.
- Love moves us to help and serve others.
- Love is the most powerful force in the universe.
- Love is a choice, but it's also a verb, which is realized through our actions and service.
- Love is the single greatest motivator. It is the "Why" behind everything.

> "For God so loved the world that He gave His only begotten Son that whoever believes in Him shall not perish, but have eternal life." – JOHN 3:16

The more you exercise your choice to love,
the more capacity for love you build. The happiness that comes from sharing your journey energizes you.

When I arrived at Georgia Tech, **the only people I knew in the entire state were the coaches.** That first Sunday, I put on a clean T-shirt and my jeans. It was February, but I didn't own a winter coat.

It took me two hours to figure out Atlanta's public transportation system and make my way to church across town on Ponce de Leon. I arrived at the small chapel an hour early.

During the service Don Conkey sat next to me. Afterwards he and his wife, Joan, invited me to their home for brunch. An older couple with grown children, the Conkeys lived in an old mansion on Oxford Road in Druid Hills, near where *Driving Miss Daisy* was filmed. **Their world couldn't have been more different from the one I'd left behind, but they didn't hesitate to welcome me into it.**

"You have family here,"

said Don, who gave me a ride back to my dorm. *"Here's our number. If you need anything, call me. There's always a haven here if you need to get away."*

The enormity of this complete stranger offering his home to me and using the word "family" made a powerful, lasting impact in my life and still moves me to tears whenever I think about that moment.

That simple act of kindness—the extension of love and hospitality—from a perfect stranger meant the world to me. His words and actions changed me forever.

I figured out the bus route to their house. A successful businessman and a deeply spiritual person, **Don invested his time in me and Joan became like a mother to me.** On the weekends, I'd often take a bus from the campus in downtown Atlanta to their quiet, tree-lined street with its stately, grand homes. The Conkeys offered me a safe place on my journey. And when I awoke from my surgeries, Joan was keeping a vigil at my hospital bedside.

Since I didn't have anything to go home to in the summers, I lived with the Conkeys. Don was the person who helped me with my decision to change my path and become a missionary rather than pursuing my pro football career.

If I hadn't made that decision, I never would have met the beautiful young woman who lived in Canada and eventually became my wife.

My kids now refer to the Conkeys as their grandparents, and I still seek their counsel on vital decisions. I'm so grateful that they've served as some of my guides on this journey.

LOVE

"Tell me what is it that you plan to do with your one wild and precious life?" – MARY OLIVER

f course, in the end, nobody can motivate you to make radical changes. **Lasting change must be ignited from within.** You have to love yourself enough to move in a positive direction. **Think about how you talk to yourself** – your thoughts and inner dialogue. Would you want to be stuck on a long vacation with that person? If you're in the habit of being hypercritical of yourself, work on replacing negative self-talk with positive thoughts.

"True love can alter human lives and change human nature." – THOMAS S. MONSON

Radical lasting change simply cannot happen without deep, devoted, honest, true love. **Love does not just spark on its own.** To allow love to work its power in your life, you must reach out to others – people who share it without expectation. I know trusting can be the hardest thing in the world when you've been hurt and disappointed. But trust me when I say that LOVE changes everything. Authentic and genuine love is the most powerful force in the universe.

The important question is: How do we receive it, give it and bask in it? **Love allows everyone around us to flourish and grow.**

As a young adult, my self worth was virtually non-existent. One day at practice, during my red-shirt sophomore year in college, I hit the wall emotionally. **I collapsed under the weight of suffering years of abuse,** being at one of the country's most academically challenging schools and fighting to re-earn my starting position. I woke up in the hospital.

Coach Curry loved me enough to get me the professional help I needed. In the boiling pressure cooker of major college football in the South, coaches are under so much duress to produce a winning team that few would have taken the time that he did to help get to the root of my problems. Coach Curry sent me to two psychiatrists. Dr. Barbara Winship became my tour guide in a safe place of healing.

She started me on the journey to get past the abuse. Dr. Terry Maple **helped me with my performance on the field,** using biofeedback for pain management and visualization to help me improve.

It's kind of like going to see a mechanic. If something is wrong, you may keep driving a little while, but eventually your car will break down. It's better to get it fixed right in the first place, instead of sputtering along. **Don't be afraid to make a pit stop and get a professional tune-up.**

The way you see yourself has a direct and dramatic impact on what you accomplish in your life and whether you enjoy your journey. **LET LOVE GUIDE YOUR STEPS.**

What motivates you to change?

Many people I've met have been motivated by a **negative emotion such as fear or anger.** However, when you're fueled by the negative, **you eventually flame out.** For example, if you have a heart attack due to being overweight and decide to make lifestyle changes, which would motivate you more: a fear of dying or a desire to live a full and joyous life? Fear can be a powerful motivator for a little while but for the long haul, **you need to focus on the positive. Love conquers fear. Let love be the "WHY" behind each of your goals.**

We all need guides. We need many friends and mentors to help us along the path to our best selves. Keep your eyes open for those special people who know the best routes, the shortcuts, and the fun side trips that you'd never discover without them by your side.

How will
you change?

Who will help you?

Write down one or two people who serve (or could serve) as your **guide** or **mentor** in all of these areas:

Spiritually

Mentally

Emotionally

Physically

Initiate special time
with each person. Meet as consistently
as their schedules allow.

Write down 10 things that you
like most about yourself.

Look at this list on a daily
basis if you struggle with
negative self-talk.

Write down the name of a person
whom you've allowed to block
your forward progress.

How can you
limit that person's
influence on your life?

Write down the name of a friend
or family member who encourages
you in each of the areas listed
on the previous page.

Spend the bulk of your free time surrounding yourself with *encouragers.*

CHANGE

"Nobody can go back and start a new beginning, but anyone can start today and make a new ending."
— MARIA ROBINSON

Enjoy the journey.

To be a good traveler, you've got to be adaptable. Weather and schedules change. The food may be different from what you're used to. You may encounter delays or detours, or the route you've mapped out may be blocked unexpectedly.

REMEMBER:
"It is not the strongest of the species that survives, nor the most intelligent, but the ones most responsive to change." – CHARLES DARWIN

THE GIFT
the ability to change
is right in front of you. Open the box.
Now think and LIVE outside that box.

Radical change is power.
That power lives in your soul.

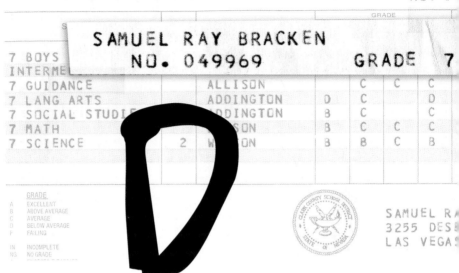

The only true constant in life is that everything changes constantly. When most people talk about change, they encourage you to take baby steps. *"Change just a few things at a time, so you won't get discouraged."* You don't see magazine articles or TV shows about someone who loses 5 pounds. Add a "0" to that 5 and then you'll see a person's efforts celebrated. Nobody gets inspired by miniscule changes.

Radical change requires radical choices. When you are radical about change, you build momentum. Producing quick wins encourages you to keep moving ahead.

CREATE A CHANGE REVOLUTION IN YOUR LIFE.

CHANGE

How do you do that? Constantly keep your vision sharply in focus in your mind's eye, and above all, aim high.

"Shoot for the moon. Even if you miss, you'll land among the stars."

— LES BROWN

After I finally got into mainstream classes as a high school freshman, **I set a goal of graduating with straight As** at the top of my class of more than 700 students.

Given my academic success up until that point that goal was pretty audacious. **Many nights I didn't even know where I was going to lay my head** since I was bouncing from place to place. My older stepbrothers and stepsisters all dropped out of high school. I'd been a C and D special ed student and had a lot of catching up to do. If the bookies in Vegas were taking bets on me, I would have been a long shot.

CHANGE

But I knew that to bolster my chance at my dream of becoming a pro football player, **I needed to earn a college scholarship.** My friend, Brian Cross, warned me that even if I had the talent as a football player, being a poor student would come back to haunt me as it did him.

Of the more than 1 million high school football players, **only .01 percent score a Division I football scholarship,** and of college players, fewer than 2 percent go on to play pro. I didn't care about the odds.

Having a goal that most people would have viewed as completely out of my reach inspired me to spend hours and hours studying. **I worked harder than my peers to get the grades I got.** And because I dreamed of signing that pro football contract, I spent extra hours in the weight room. I also ran everywhere.

I RAN THE STADIUM STAIRS.

I RAN TO WORK.

I RAN TO SCHOOL.

I RAN IN THE DESERT.

R.
89

SAMUEL RAY BRACKEN
NO. D49969   GRADE 12

HASE	TEACHER	GRADE				CITIZENSHIP		ABSENCES			CREDITS
		PERIOD		EXAM	FINAL	PERIOD		PERIOD		SEM.	
		1	2			1	2	1	2		
	BRILLE J	A	A	A	A	S	E	08	09	17	0.500
	JOHNSTON D	A	A	A	A	E	E	03	07	10	0.500
	SAGERS D	B	A	A	A	E	E	11	11	22	0.500
	SPENCER G	B	A	A	A	S	S	02	09	11	0.500

"Dreams and goals are the coming attractions in your life." — JOSEPH CAMPBELL

EA

IOD

Guess what happened to the kid who had languished in special education classes for eight years? I didn't become valedictorian. **But I graduated with a 3.95 GPA and ranked number 11 out of more than 700 students at Chaparral High School.**

The chasm I had to overcome threatened to engulf me. It scared me, and I knew I couldn't do it alone.

So I reached up and reached out. I asked for help from caring teachers, friends and their parents. I held myself accountable to change while key friends, mentors and coaches who loved me kept me accountable.

I radically changed the way I approached school and my work ethic in order to bridge that vast gap in my life.

How did I make such big changes? Change requires discipline and a focus on new behavior.

I focused on **changing the behavior** that would help me **reach my goal.**

Each day I was disciplined about behaving in a way that I thought would produce the results I was after.

Although I always kept my goal in mind, I didn't obsess over the dream. **Obsessing can lock you up and overwhelm you.** Focus on the daily efforts that will produce the desired results. Break down specifics that will lead you to your goal. Daily effort around the specific new behavior is a sure bet. It gives you the best chance to reach your goal.

"How we spend our days is how we spend our lives."
— ANNIE DILLARD

Focusing on what's within your control frees you.

Changing your own behavior is something you can act on daily, and you can track your progress.

What if I'd set a more modest goal of graduating with a C average? I can tell you right now that Georgia Tech wouldn't have recruited me.

DO IT

If you're going to do something,

BIG!

6

CHANGE

That seemingly impossible dream goal

of being a straight A student catapulted me ahead
on what I now believe was the path destined for me.

*Even if you get only part of
the way to where you want
to go you'll be much farther
along than most people.*

W hen I got to Georgia Tech, I continued to
pursue being a great student as well as a
great football player. Once again I set my
goal high: straight As. I soon found out
that hardly any of the 15,000 students at Georgia
Tech make straight As. But I didn't let that quell
my desire. I still kept plugging away.

After I suffered what appeared to be career-ending shoulder injuries, my scholarship wasn't in danger because of the institution's commitment to the student athlete. However, because I'd poured myself into my academic studies as well as football during my last two years at Georgia Tech, **I moved from an athletic scholarship to an academic one, which offered me even more benefits.**

Although I wasn't named an All American for my football prowess, I was recognized for both my intellectual and athletic talent as Academic All Conference my junior and senior years. And I was also nominated for the *Brian Piccolo Award* for coming back from my injuries. **Those weren't my ultimate goals, but you better believe that I was thrilled with those honors as I continued my journey.**

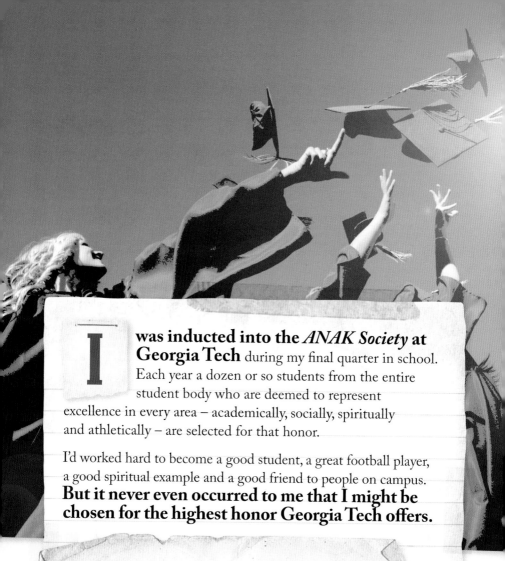

I was inducted into the *ANAK Society* at **Georgia Tech** during my final quarter in school. Each year a dozen or so students from the entire student body who are deemed to represent excellence in every area – academically, socially, spiritually and athletically – are selected for that honor.

I'd worked hard to become a good student, a great football player, a good spiritual example and a good friend to people on campus. **But it never even occurred to me that I might be chosen for the highest honor Georgia Tech offers.**

Aiming high took me to a marvelous, unexpected place.

Once again, I didn't quite make my goal of straight As, but **I graduated with honors from Georgia Tech,** one of the nation's most academically challenging schools.

The difference between good and great is miniscule. At 211 degrees water is just water. But at 212 degrees it turns into steam that can power a locomotive. Often times, it's just a little more work, a little higher aspiration, slightly more focus that will propel you along your path.

My point is that you never can tell what the results will be of shooting for the moon.

Just remember to savor the journey along the way.

- Have fun.
- Delight in the unexpected views.
- Taste the unusual foods and marvel at the different customs you encounter.

Enjoy your adventure.

c 76541

Focus on the thinking you need to change in order to reach your dream destination.

Keep your dream destination in mind, but understand that your thinking affects **the behavior that is your day-to-day measuring stick** to let you know if you're making progress on your journey.

Keeping score on your behavior leads to big changes. For example, if I just focus on the negative thought that I'm overweight and out of shape, I'm much less likely to stick to the plan that will allow me to reach my overall goal of losing 30 pounds. That mindset is discouraging. However, if I see food as fuel and see myself on a journey to better health and more fun with my family, **sticking to the plan becomes far easier.** If I track every day what I'm eating and how much I'm exercising, I can see my progress.

What behavior do you need to change in order to reach your goal?

Track your progress on a daily basis in a notebook or on the computer. Use whatever tool works for you, but keep score!

Don't be concerned when you have to make a detour or reach a roadblock. Figure out how to adapt. Radical change will take you places you never imagined.

TRAVEL TIP 151332

Get your guides and traveling companions to help you become accountable for the changes you want to make. Make adjustments to your course as needed. Celebrate your victories whenever you reach specific mile markers along your journey.

6 CHANGE

How will you
reach your destination?

179

What change **are you resisting**
right now?

Write down some
unexpected benefits
of a change you've made.

If you tackle the *boldest goal* on your list,

name **5** *good things* that might happen as a result.

GRATITUDE

"Justice demands that we seek and find the stranger, the broken, the prisoner, and comfort them and offer them our help. Here lies the holy compassion of God."
— MECHTILD OF MAGDEBURG

Share your adventures.

When you go on an incredible journey, what's the first thing you do when you arrive home? You share your adventures – your stories, your experiences, your lessons learned and your photos from your trip.

One of the most important things you can do as you move forward on your path is SHARE YOUR ADVENTURES.

Doing that helps you to be grateful for your traveling companions and guides who accompanied you. It reminds you of all the wonderful places you've been and the excitement you felt when you overcame hardships along the way.

Be willing to help others find their paths. Because I am so grateful for the many people who have helped me, I reach for others to help them along their journeys.

The best adventures always contain the **unexpected.** Finding your way out of a difficult spot adds to your growth and self-esteem. Being grateful for all things – even the detours, bumps and delays – is another radical choice that we are called to make. I am grateful for all that I've overcome and encountered on my journey, because it's led me to the place where I am today.

When you feel grateful for the bad things that have set you back, you have arrived at a place of emotional healing and peace that leads to happiness.

That gratitude allowed me to have compassion for my mother and embrace her despite the pain her poor choices had caused in me. **None of us can truly be joyous without love and forgiveness.**

Gratitude is evidence that you've packed your bag right.

I know that without my guides and traveling companions I could have ended up in a very different place.

O ver the last several years, I've devoted a good deal of my time to kids who are having a hard time in life. Many of them have bounced from foster home to foster home.

One young man especially stands out in my mind. Every Sunday and Wednesday night for three years, I visited kids who were incarcerated at the Decker Lake Maximum Security Youth Prison in West Valley, Utah. The kids there had been convicted of serious crimes ranging from murder to rape to armed robbery.
The number who returned to jail after release topped 99 percent.

When he was 13 years old, Jose was part of an armed robbery where a convenience store clerk was gunned down and killed. Jose and his 19-year-old buddy made off with a carton of cigarettes and $5. For three years, I met with Jose, hoping to help him have a breakthrough and become aware of how he might change.

"Yo, Sam," he said one Sunday after I shared my whole story with him. ***"I have these thoughts about what I'd do on the outside. If I saw some punk from one of our rivals, I'd like to gut him."*** He went into gory detail about what he'd do to the other gang member. **I think he expected me to be shocked.**

"Jose, based on how you grew up and the fact that you've been in a gang since you were age six, those thoughts are perfectly normal," I said. *"You've been hardwired to think that way. My hardwiring was all messed up, too. What matters is what you do with those thoughts. You may not be able to control random thoughts that pop into your mind.*

What you can control is what you do with that thought once it's in your brain.

You can replace it with affirmations of a great future, with thoughts of love and kindness, with positive music.

There are many good things with which you can replace the bad thoughts."

I saw his face light up.

"Nobody has ever told me that," he said. *"I can control my thinking?"*

"Yes, you can train yourself to think differently. Most people don't guard their thoughts. You've got to protect your thinking against the bad. **Your mind is a sacred place. Protect it always.** *The journey to change your behavior and reach your goals begins in your mind."*

I could see the light of hope in Jose's eyes that day.

I saw something else when I looked at Jose. **I saw where I could have so easily wound up if I hadn't made that radical choice when I was his age to:**

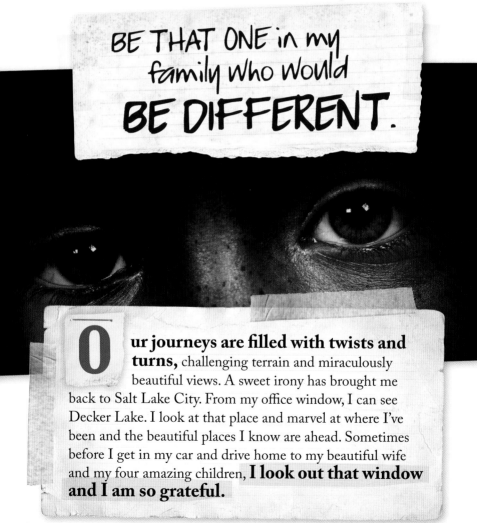

BE THAT ONE in my family who would BE DIFFERENT.

Our journeys are filled with twists and **turns,** challenging terrain and miraculously beautiful views. A sweet irony has brought me back to Salt Lake City. From my office window, I can see Decker Lake. I look at that place and marvel at where I've been and the beautiful places I know are ahead. Sometimes before I get in my car and drive home to my beautiful wife and my four amazing children, **I look out that window and I am so grateful.**

For many years I thought that my own sheer dogged determination and hard work were the secrets behind my success. Today I realize those things only got me started. But it was the people – the beautiful, kind, generous, caring and loving people in my life who served and saved me.

True meaningful change is impossible on your own. I would not have the life I have now without the help of so many people.

So I ask you to reach out and across. Reach down. Reach up.

At the end of my journey, I know what will fill my orange duffel bag: *the relationships I've nurtured all along the way, gratitude for where I've been and the*

peace, joy, love & happiness that I've found.

Your brain doesn't know the difference between fact or fiction.

Affirm the state you want to be in, and pretend you are already there. **Think of positive affirmations as your passport to the marvelous places you want to go.** See how many stamps you can get in your passport. Now express your gratitude for each success as if it's already happened.

We become what we think about most.

When we are filled with gratitude for those who helped us along the path, the view from wherever we are looks so much better.

TRAVEL TIP 151332

Have fun with this exercise. Video yourself affirming your goals and watch it everyday. Use images and words that mean something to you.

Where will your
passport take you?

Use Affirmations daily.

Mental Affirmation

Physical Affirmation

Emotional Affirmation

Spiritual Affirmation

ARE YOU THERE YET?

HINT: The answer is **NO**

When you think you have arrived, you are in trouble. Stay true to the great journey mapped out for you. **Remember and review the 7 Rules for the Road often.**

Georgia Tech™

I can't wait
to see where my orange
duffel bag goes with me next.

Celebrate the journey,
Sam Bracken

P.S. Share your adventures
with me at **MyOrangeDuffelBag.com.**
I'd love to hear from you.

And continue your journey with

My Roadmap: A Personal Guide to Balance, Power, and Purpose
($9.99; Canada: $11.99; 978-0-307-95586-9)

Available wherever books are sold

My gratitude

for my mother, Clara Pearl Holloway, who made more changes in her lifetime than I thought humanly possible, and for all the wonderful people who have reached out to help me make radical changes in my life

KIM BRACKEN, BEAU BRACKEN,
BEN BRACKEN, JAKE BRACKEN, HANNAH BRACKEN,
GERALD BRACKEN, CATHY BRACKEN, LEROY BRACKEN,
ROY BRACKEN, ANN BRACKEN, SABRINA BRACKEN, KEN BLAIR,
BILL & CAROLYN CURRY, BRIAN CROSS, JOHN CHURA, KIM KING,
MAC MCWHORTER, ANDY HEARN, DREW HEARN, CHARLIE JONES,
KIMBERLY CETRON, SEAN COVEY, STEPHEN R. COVEY, BOB WHITMAN,
TODD STANSBURY, HOMER RICE, DON & JOAN CONKEY, FRED CARILLO,
MICHAEL SIMPSON, LAVELL EDWARDS, DALE MURPHY, JOHN PORTER,
PETE & CINDY RICHARDS, JENNIFER COONS, JENNIFER COLOSIMO,
GLENN TUCKETT, BRADLEY MILLER, JOHN HARDY, NANCY HARDY,
RUSSELL BALLARD, LYNN ELKINS, PHIL & PAM KARSKI,
JON BRILLE, DARNELL FRAZIER, MARC VALDOV, TOM LAPE,
DEBBIE & BRENT JORGENSEN, BOB & MARYLOU ORME,
HARVEY & ARLEEN LANGFORD, DONA HALE LAKIS,
BRENT ORME, PAT STEVENS, MIKE DALY, MONTE RAY,
BART OATS, RANDY & AMANDA THORDERSON,
SAM ALLMAN, CHRIS DECHRISTO,
REX PINEGAR, TAZ ANDERSON,
ERIK & JANA FULLER,
KEVIN MONTGOMERY,
MIKE TRAVIS,
SHAWN MOON,
ART BURGE,

JEFF SWANSON,
BERNARD & KAREN DUKE,
MARIA & DICK SULLIVAN, OWEN THOMAS,
CARRIE & MIKE OLSEN, CLIVE & BONNIE ROMNEY,
GREG & JODY WADDOUPS, SISSY WALLACE, KEN & KIM CARNEY,
BLAIR WILLIAMS, RICK & KATHY BARTON, MONTE THORNTON,
JEFF DAVIS, SHASHI CAAN, DEAN COLLINWOOD, FATIMA DOMAN,
BRUCE & JOYCE EDWARDS, SHELLY GAITHER, SHERMAN & TAMMY GARDNER,
BOB FISK, ROBERT & KAREN NIEDZWIECKI, JOHN GARFF, MICHELE L. STUMPE,
WADE THOMAS, CATHY PERRY, KATHY HERREN, EBONY HARRIS, MARVIS TUTIAH,
KATHY LOUISE PATRICK & THE PULPWOOD QUEENS, ELIZABETH MORRELL,
VIRGINIA MELDRUM, CARL BOUCKAERT, CONNOR GARRETT, SARAH NOBLE,
LEIGH STEVENS, ANNIE OSWALD, MICHELLE WARD, PAULA PARRISH,
CALEB GARRETT, JON & AMANDA SWINDALL, DAMIEN BURKE, SHANE
& DEBBIE STEVENS, STUART DICKSON, KEVIN CRONK, KRIS SIDDOWAY,
CARINE CLARK, DAVID DENHAM, ANDREW WELCH, FRED ALLMAN,
CHRIS MCKEE, CHRIS YANDOW, LARRY OLSEN, JERI ROBERTS, NEIL TEITSMA,
B.J. WALKER, DOUG & DIANE MOFFATT, JACQUELINE ONTIVEROS,
LAURA JOHNSON, MATT MURDOCH, COURTNEY MATTSON, JOE BUSHÉY,
TERRY MAPLE, BARBARA WINSHIP, BILL MCDONALD, MARK ALBERT,
DAVE PASSENELLA, JOHN IVEMEYER, GREG HILLMEYER, JODY KARR,
MARILYN MCSWEENY, LAWTON HYDRICK, JOHN MANNION, PHIL ADLER,
IRVIN KRISS, CLAYTON SAMPSON, BISHOP NORDA, PENNY HALE,
BRUCE WHEELER, BRENT KUIK, CINDY HUNSINGER, JAN MILLER,
NENA MADONIA, JULIA PASTORE, MICHAEL PALGON, TINA CONSTABLE,
SUSAN BROWN, NATASHA BOLDEN, LAURA WATTS, DAVID & JANE
KARANGU, ANGELA LEE, DIANA BLACK, MARK & DEE DEE COOLEY,
SCOTT PATRICK, PERNESSA SEELE, ARLETTE MURRAIN,
JEFF WADSWORTH, TODD KROSTEWITZ, AMY MULLIS,
JEFF & SUSAN SOUTH, ECHO & KEVIN GARRETT,
RICHARD BECKER, RAY KUIK....

The Orange Duffel Bag Foundation—a 501c3 nonprofit cofounded by Sam Bracken and Echo Garrett—is dedicated to providing professional life coaching, training and advocacy for youth in foster care and at-risk and homeless youth to help them become self-reliant. Join us in bringing hope, meaning and change to our at-risk youth, ages 12–24. A portion of the proceeds from *My Orange Duffel Bag* goes to support the Orange Duffel Bag Foundation (ODBF). Here's how you can help with our mission:

1. ODBF has partnered with Every Child USA to raise awareness and funds to support our work. With your cell phone, you can donate $10 by texting the word ORANGE to 85944. Reply YES when prompted and your donation will be charged on your phone bill.

2. Donate $500 to sponsor a case of *My Orange Duffel Bag* books, which will allow us to give them to a group home for youth in foster care. Reading the book will be the first step on their journey to radical change.

3. A $2,500 donation provides an at-risk youth with our full 12-week professional life coaching. Upon graduation, each young person receives an orange duffel bag filled with useful items and is matched with an ODBF advocate, a caring adult who helps assist the ODBF graduate on his or her journey.

www.OrangeDuffelBagFoundation.org
Toll-free number in US: 800-598-5150
Email: OrangeDuffelBagFoundation@gmail.com
Facebook: www.facebook.com/pages/Orange-Duffel-Bag-Foundation/138001609577884
Twitter: @ODBFoundation, twitter.com/#!/ODBFoundation

Sam Bracken is available for select readings and lectures.

To inquire about a possible appearance, please visit www.rhspeakers.com or call 212-572-2013.

For group or corporate coaching and training based on Sam's *7 Rules for the Road,* please contact him at sbracken@mac.com.

My Orange Duffel Bag is the proud recipient of

2011 Outstanding Book of the Year in the Young Adult/Children's category, the American Society of Journalists and Authors

2011 Merit Award for Editorial Design, from *HOW* magazine

2011 Benjamin Franklin Book Award Silver Medalist in both Self-Help and Juvenile/Young Adult Nonfiction categories, the Independent Book Publishers Association

2011 IPPY Gold Medal for Most Outstanding Design, the Independent Publishers Book Awards

2011 National Indie Excellence Book Awards Winner, New Nonfiction and Young Adult Nonfiction categories

SAM BRACKEN serves as the national spokesperson for the Orange Duffel Bag Foundation. He is also general manager of FranklinCovey Media Publishing, a division of the world's foremost training and leadership development company operating in 147 countries. A member of the National Speakers Association, Sam graduated Georgia Tech with honors and received his MBA from Brigham Young University's Marriott School of Management. He and his wife, Kim, live in the Rocky Mountains with their four children.

 www.facebook.com/pages/Sam-Bracken/208860949175067?sk=wall

 @SamBracken67; twitter.com/#!/sambracken67

 SBracken67; www.youtube.com/user/sbracken67

ECHO GARRETT, a journalist with 30 years' experience, is author of *Why Don't They Just Get a Job? One Couple's Mission to End Poverty in Their Community, Dream No Little Dreams,* and several other books. Formerly Editor-in-Chief of *Atlanta Woman,* Echo has been published in more than 75 national publications and appeared on *Good Morning America,* CNBC, CNN, and NY-1. She holds a journalism degree from Auburn University. Echo and her husband, Kevin Garrett, a photographer who contributed most of the images in this book, have two sons, Caleb and Connor, and reside in metro Atlanta. She cofounded the Orange Duffel Bag Foundation and works to supports its mission.

www.echogarrett.com

 Facebook: www.facebook.com/pages/Echo-Garrett/155148734571077?sk=wall

 Twitter: @echogarrett; twitter.com/#!/echogarrett

MyOrangeDuffelBag.com

Follow us on Facebook:

www.facebook.com/pages/My-Orange-Duffel-Bag-A-Journey-To-Radical-Change/166020844367